Morality by Design

First published in the UK in 2019 by
Intellect, The Mill, Parnall Road, Fishponds, Bristol, BS16 3JG, UK

First published in the USA in 2019 by
Intellect, The University of Chicago Press, 1427 E. 60th Street, Chicago, IL
60637, USA

A catalogue record for this book is available from the British Library.

Copy editing: MPS Technology
Cover and Layout Design: Aleksandra Szumlas
Typesetting: Contentra
Production Manager: Tim Mitchell

Print ISBN: 978-1-78938-123-8
ePDF ISBN: 978-1-78938-125-2
ePUB ISBN: 978-1-78938-124-5

Printed & bound by Severn, Gloucester, UK.

To find out about all our publications, please visit
www.intellectbooks.com
There, you can subscribe to our e-newsletter,
browse or download our current catalogue,
and buy any titles that are in print.

This is a peer-reviewed publication.

Morality by Design

Technology's Challenge to Human Values

BY

Wade Rowland

Bristol, UK / Chicago, USA

Books by Wade Rowland:

Canada Lives Here: The Case For Public Broadcasting

Greed, Inc.: Why Corporations Rule Our World and How We Let It Happen

Spirit of the Web: The Age of Information from Telegraph to Internet

Galileo's Mistake: The Archaeology of a Myth

Ockham's Razor: A Search for Wonder in an Age of Doubt

The Plot to Save the World: The Life and Times of the Stockholm Conference on the Human Environment

For Chris and her violet light

When a well-clothed philosopher on a bitter winter's night sits in a warm room well lighted for his purpose and writes on paper with pen and ink in the arbitrary characters of a highly developed language the statement that civilisation is the result of natural laws, and that man's duty is to let nature alone so that untrammeled it may work out a higher civilisation, he simply ignores every circumstance of his existence and deliberately closes his eyes to every fact within the range of his faculties. If man had acted upon his theory there would have been no civilisation, and our philosopher would have remained a troglodyte.

Lester Ward, *Mind*, Vol. IX (1884)

Two things fill the mind with ever new and increasing admiration and reverence, the more often and more steadily one reflects on them: the starry heavens above me and the moral law within me.

Immanuel Kant, *Critique of Pure Reason* (1788)

Contents

Introduction

1

How do you build a utopia? What does it take to construct the best of all possible worlds? Thomas More chose the name 'Utopia' (in Greek, it means 'no-place') for the ideal society he described in his Renaissance masterpiece of 1516, written as a young man long before he served as Lord Chancellor to Henry VIII (and was beheaded for his trouble). The book was a visionary critique of fractious English society, which More described as a 'conspiracy of the rich', where the 'greedy, unscrupulous and useless' lived off the labour of others. In *Utopia*, he sketched a form of radical socialism as the solution to the inequities he saw around him. In his imaginary island society, communal farms shared their surpluses, and hours of work were kept to a minimum in order to allow plenty of time for leisure and education. Human dignity took precedence over money and prestige, and laws were so simple that there was no need for lawyers.

A hundred years later, a new era had dawned in Europe, bringing with it radical new ways of thinking about truth and meaning. A very different utopia was envisioned by a new breed of political and economic thinkers. It would be based on revolutionary rationalist, scientific and individualist ideals that were emphatically opposed to the 'outdated' philosophies of Greece and Rome that had inspired More and his Renaissance peers. Like so many of today's Silicon Valley idealists, these self-styled Enlightenment theorists hoped to create a more perfect world through the power of pure reason and individual liberty unencumbered by irrational religious belief and speculative moral theory, a power made concrete and activated through science and technology.

The Enlightenment world-view would eventually lead us to our current reality, justly celebrated for stupendous material wealth and astounding scientific and technical progress on all fronts. But accompanying these achievements, entwined with them, are disturbing trends: monumental environmental catastrophes, and an alarming moral ethos in which human beings are reduced to the status of 'consumers', 'data-points', 'human resources' and 'human capital'.

2

In trying to create a more perfect world, a handful of brilliant, well-intentioned economic and political thinkers of the seventeenth and eighteenth centuries set in motion dynamics that have led to a global economy ruled over by gargantuan, machine-like business corporations that treat humanity as a renewable natural resource, a means to material ends.

In the 'more perfect' world that has evolved out of these early rationalist ideas, the processes of automation, machine learning, and artificial intelligence are pushing more and more people into precarious, part-time work, while most of the vast wealth generated by the resultant efficiencies goes to a tiny, obscenely wealthy minority.

The system has begun to feed on those it was created to serve. Having despoiled much of the planet through reckless economic expansion and ruthless exploitation of natural resources, it is now turning to humans themselves to supply the raw material of continued growth. Technology has invaded social relations, inserting itself between the flesh-and-blood people of communities and mediating their communication for profit. The world's most valuable resource is no longer oil – it's data: data about all sorts of things and processes, but mostly about people, our tastes and interests, our likes and dislikes, our entertainment preferences and shopping habits, and our online activities.[1] That data is collected from our phones and computers, our wristwatches and our cars and even from our robotic vacuum cleaners and refrigerators. Much of it is proffered by us voluntarily, as we take advantage of 'free' social media platforms to communicate with one another.

In this context, the term 'human resources', a twentieth-century coinage, takes on a new and ominous meaning: each of us has a new kind of commodity-value that is wrapped up in the data-trail we produce as we go about our lives within the information ecosystem, using our ever-smarter digital devices. As that ecosystem expands continuously to occupy more and more life-space, the tyranny of convenience ensures that we relinquish more and more privacy and autonomy as we generate the raw resource that is the lifeblood of the new digital economy.[2] The digital economy is becoming a vast dairy farm, in which humans are the placid, profit-generating livestock.

In the information economy, we ourselves – our bodies, our genes, our amusements, our relationships, and most of all, our attention – are the golden fleece out of which capital is spun. At the same time, on-the-job conditions for workers are steadily deteriorating, with precarious employment, longer and longer hours, just-in-time scheduling, low pay, and relentless electronic surveillance causing an epidemic of stress-related mental and physical illness.[3] As we become justifiably alarmed at the depletion, exhaustion and pollution of the natural resources that fuelled the success of market capitalism, we might well ask: does the same fate await *us*, as *human* resources? Do information theory and computer-based technologies, operating in a market-capitalist environment, threaten human sustainability? Was there a fatal flaw built into ideas of those early economists and political thinkers who bequeathed to us 'scientific' market capitalism and its ideological justifications?

3

These issues are raised afresh in today's excited talk of 'the singularity', a transformative moment in human history, coming sometime in the mid-twenty-first century according to futurist Ray Kurzweil and others. It will mark the arrival and widespread application of machine super-intelligence that outstrips human capabilities, and it is described as an inevitable near-future in which humans are reduced to serfdom in the service of omnipotent, omniscient technological systems to which they have ceded control. Less dystopic but equally preposterous, in my view, are the more 'optimistic' proselytizers of trans-humanism, the genetic engineers who ardently advocate a technologically perfected human race, super-brainy, disease-free, perfectly socialized.

Whatever we may think of these radical speculations, the fact remains that, as we struggle to cope with the terrible toll our economic successes have taken on the natural environment, we are now forced to deal with some challenging new issues. The question facing us is: what is it about being human that we want to preserve, to protect from the seductions of technology and the market? What exactly is at risk when we deploy engineering strategies to 'improve' humanity and its social environment? What might a 'perfected' human being be like? What limits should be imposed on the infiltration and manipulation of human life and activity by machine intelligence?

As is the case with more traditional environmental issues, these are moral questions, difficult and time-consuming to wrestle with. They demand both philosophical scrutiny and extended political debate. Unfortunately, we have all but lost the vocabulary of moral discourse, and consequently have little confidence in our ability to make sound moral judgements for reasons this book will explore. Meanwhile, the trans-humanists, for their part, are offering up a shining path to a tomorrow in which people are stronger, healthier, more perfectly formed, more intelligent, perhaps even immortal. A future in which perceived human frailties and shortcomings have been transcended and utopia is finally realized. All we have to do is carry on with the status quo, standing aside to allow instrumental reason to continue to work the mechanical magic we have learned to call 'progress'. It's a lopsided contest.

The purpose of this volume is to provide, in an informal way, some of the relevant context for this necessary debate, and some of the language and tools of contemporary moral philosophy that can help make sense of the issues. In particular, it provides an introduction to an approach to moral reflection and discourse called 'critical moral realism', which is both as old as philosophy and as relevant as the latest speculations in quantum physics. Along the way, it will exhume and dust off some remarkably persistent ideas that have been deposited in the sediments of conventional wisdom across four hundred years of Western history. Although these ideas continue to animate (one might say, *infect*) the liberal capitalist democracies of today, the moral and historical contexts that spawned them are seldom examined. That needs to change, if we are to avoid being railroaded into a future in which what is best in humanity is sacrificed on the altar of an irresponsible, thoughtless pursuit of the technologically possible, which we mistakenly call progress.

Chapter 1:

The Idea of Science

1

The economist John Maynard Keynes spoke of our civilization being decisively shaped by the enduring power of the ideas, good and bad, of political philosophers and economists of earlier times. Writing in 1936, he said: 'Practical men, who believe themselves to be quite exempt from any intellectual influences, are usually the slaves of some defunct economist. Madmen in authority, who hear voices in the air, are distilling their frenzy from some academic scribbler of a few years back'.[4] Twenty years later, Keynes' worthy successor, John Kenneth Galbraith, coined the term 'conventional wisdom' to describe the unthinking acceptance of embedded dogma, biases and prejudices, or as he put it, 'the beliefs that are at any time assiduously, solemnly, and mindlessly traded between the pretentiously wise'.[5] He told a biographer he intended the term to be 'overtly respectful but with an undertone of disdain, even ridicule. Something nicely balanced between approval and ridicule'. I can do no better than to take my cue from these great men, and begin this exploration of the pitfalls of 'progress' with the English philosopher and political theorist Thomas Hobbes, a prolific scribbler and proto-economist whose political and economic ideas have shown themselves to be extraordinarily tenacious despite their obvious shortcomings. Born amid the terror and confusion of the aborted Spanish invasion of Elizabethan England in 1588, he was an early adopter of the radical materialist thinking that characterized the scientific revolution at the heart of what history would call variously the Enlightenment and 'the Age of Reason'.

The son of a Protestant pastor, Hobbes subscribed to a flinty individualism in which there was little room for charity. A well-to-do uncle staked him to a decent education culminating at Oxford, where he learned to hate conventional philosophy with its roots in Aristotle and its boundaries prescribed in Roman Catholic theology. As a bright young scholar he became tutor to the son of a rich and well-connected English family, and was able to travel widely with his pupil in Europe: he met with Galileo Galilei, then under Vatican-imposed house arrest in his villa outside the walls of Florence; and in Paris he met radical anti-clerical thinkers who were beginning to work out the foundations of the modern scientific world-view, men like the essayist Michel de Montaigne, astronomer Pierre Gassendi, mathematician Marin Mersenne, and the philosopher René Descartes. Back home in England, in the 1620s Hobbes worked as secretary and translator for another of the founders of modern science, Francis Bacon.

Hobbes would survive the tumult of the English Civil Wars (1640–51), the execution of Charles I and the restoration of the monarchy; the vicious religious warfare that roiled Europe during the Reformation and Counter-Reformation; an outbreak of bubonic plague that carried away a quarter of the population of London (1665–66), and the Great Fire that followed and destroyed much of the central city over three days and nights. The tumult of his times seems to have darkened his outlook on the human condition.

In general, though, the intellectual milieu in which Hobbes would become a leading figure was fresh and radical, so much so that the period is identified with the birth of Modernity. The Protestant Reformation led by Luther and Calvin had ended the long era of the Vatican's absolute intellectual and moral authority in Europe, creating a vacuum in which new and unorthodox approaches to understanding nature and humanity could find expression. In the free-thinking climate that developed, the ability to reason was taken to be the defining feature of that new object of admiration, the self-sufficient individual. Reason was also declared to be the sole, truly reliable, source of knowledge about the world. The mysterious power of the human mind to think and form judgements logically was taken to be, was *naturalized* as, a formal system like chess or logic or mathematics, in which symbols are manipulated according to a body of rules, a kind of grammar, to produce results deemed correct or incorrect within those rules. Reason was declared to be a superior tool for decoding nature, more trustworthy, certainly, than religious texts or the surviving writings of the ancient Greeks – more reliable even than direct sensory experience, which often misled and deceived.

According to the rationalists, philosophy, understood broadly as the search for understanding of the world and humanity, ought henceforth to follow geometry in setting out its arguments and arriving at undeniable, self-evident truths. It should mimic as closely as possible the conventions and language of mathematics because ordinary, less precise language was subject to contamination by prejudices, superstitions and theological dogma, all of which the new rationalist outlook was intent on sweeping away.

There is a seductive purity about what we know (or think we know) through reason, unaffected as it is by the illusions of the senses, or the errors of ancient authorities, or the delusions of religious revelation. It is a form of knowledge that appears to be direct and unmediated, and that can be expressed in axioms of apparently unquestionable truth. Who can doubt that 2 + 2 = 4 (and not 5), or 'if A is equal to B, and B is equal to C, then A is equal to C'. Or, 'the square of the hypotenuse in a right triangle is equal to the sum of the squares of the opposite two sides?' And so by the end of the seventeenth century, not just the Christian narrative of creation but also the science of Aristotle had been undermined by the rationalist writers making waves in Paris, London, and Amsterdam, men like Descartes, Galileo, Bacon, Hobbes, and the Paris *philosophes*. In discovering mathematical patterns in nature, the early scientific explorers believed they were revealing a divine intelligence, in effect composing the texts for a 'natural religion', or 'natural philosophy', which would become simply 'science'.

2

The notions of a divinely ordained natural order, accessible to reason, and of human nature derived from that basic structure were taken up by Hobbes in his political thinking. The ideas laid out in *De Cive* (1642) and *Leviathan* (1651) reverberate down the centuries to our own time, incorporated into current economic theory and other fields such as evolutionary biology and behavioural economics. What little prosperity and security we enjoy, Hobbes said, we have *in spite of* who we are as humans. In our natural, prehistoric state, we inhabited a dog-eat-dog world in which everyone was perpetually at war with everyone else, and life was, in his famous phrase, 'solitary, poor, nasty, brutish and short'.[6] Civilization and its satisfactions, he said, have their origins in fear, which drove primitive humans to voluntarily sacrifice their freedom and independence in exchange for the security and prosperity offered by an absolute ruler, his Leviathan, capable of imposing order.

It follows that it is the rule-based order imposed, often forcibly, by our man-made institutions and not any ephemeral 'better nature' that is responsible for our ability to become civilized. Ethical decision-making, for Hobbes, is dependent on the situation at hand: where there is an absence of organized rule, we are free to do whatever it takes to save our skins; where strong authority prevails (in the form of an absolute ruler, either a king or a despot) the moral obligation is to obey the ruler. This was shockingly at odds with both ordinary human insight and theological teaching, and it led to his being vilified by many of his contemporaries.

But Hobbes was in the grip of a big idea, consumed by his ambition to develop a *theory of everything*, a grand, mechanistic model in which everything from the movements of the planets to the growth of trees to human emotions and the acquisition of knowledge could be described in terms of the same elementary materials and their interactions. Though he had no real evidence to support his theory, and had to ignore much that did not support it, the idea of the human being as an incorrigibly competitive, self-interested creature responding mechanically to external pressures and influences fit Hobbes's theory too well to be discarded.

Theory and theoretical models, in the sense of a set of general principles that operate independently of the thing explained, were certainly not new in Hobbes's day; the idea that the universe can be described in terms of geometry and mathematical ratios stretches all the way back to Pythagoras (580–500 BCE). Pythagorean thinking can be seen to varying degrees in the work of many of the philosophers of Classical and Hellenistic Greece, notably Plato and Aristotle, and the great Greco-Roman astronomer Ptolemy (100–170 CE). As Ptolemy expressed it, the point of Pythagorean, mathematics-based theorizing was to 'save the appearances' – that is, to provide an explanation of natural phenomena that rendered them measurable, calculable, and predictable. It was understood by Ptolemy that such theoretical descriptions were not to be mistaken for the reality they modelled – their function was a purely utilitarian one. For example, the value of Ptolemy's system of planetary movements, in which the unmoving Earth is at the centre of the universe, lay in its ability to predict astronomical events such as eclipses and solstices and to aid in navigation at sea, all of which it did (and does) admirably well. Ptolemaic astronomical tables were used in celestial navigation up to and beyond the time of the great seafaring explorers. Whether it was *true* or not was, for Ptolemy, another kind of question altogether.

It is in the work of Hobbes's patron Francis Bacon (1561–1626), sometimes referred to as the father of modern science, that the status of theory is explicitly elevated to truth, according the following formula: if a theory saves (i.e. provides an explanation for) all the appearances (i.e. observed phenomena), it *is* truth. In other words, a coherent theoretical, mathematical depiction of nature and its works is also a final explanation. In his *Novum Organum* Bacon says, 'There is a most intimate connection and almost an identity between the ways of human power and human knowledge. [...] That which is most useful in practice is most correct in theory'.[7]

Here, in its earliest formulations, modern science can be seen to be sliding into an intellectual rigidity amounting to dogmatism. In this intolerance lay the basis for Pope Urban VIII's epic dispute with Galileo, and the subsequent centuries of friction between religion and science. The issue was simple: science, as Galileo and many of his contemporaries understood it, was thought to be capable of providing a complete understanding of the world; the Church, however, insisted that it was only one way of knowing, and that the Judeo-Christian narrative, and moral knowledge in general, needed to be incorporated into any picture that claimed to be complete. Moral knowledge, although of a different nature than scientific knowledge, was nonetheless of equal, if not superior, validity. Moreover, the fact that a scientific theory 'works' in the sense that it is verifiable in experiments and useful in developing tools is no guarantee that it accurately depicts reality.

Neither Galileo nor Bacon was irreligious (nor for that matter was Hobbes), but Galileo in particular bridled at having to accept the Church's monopoly on intellectual authority, particularly since its teachings incorporated so much of the science of Aristotle. The Church for its part resisted, at times violently, the looming hegemony of reductionist, scientific thought – or as we now call it, Modernism.

Bacon, a more conciliatory man than Galileo, argued that the Book of Nature (detailing God's works, and accessible to reason) and the Book of God (God's will, as revealed to prophets) were complementary and inseparable texts. At the core of his enthusiasm lay his belief that progress through science and technology was the means to achieving redemption for humankind and the imminent recovery of the perfection of Eden prior to the Fall.[8]

In those beliefs, reverence of a sort is found in full measure, but contemporary critics found these new ideas to be dangerously close to a narcissistic (and heretical) reverence for man rather than God. It was a view seen to be fatally tainted with pride, which, ironically, is the sin that led to the original expulsion of Adam and Eve from Eden. The tension between faith and science would play itself out in succeeding centuries as duelling heterodoxies: each was a heresy against the other. Philosophers today sometimes frame it as a 'fact/value dichotomy'.[9]

3

An aspect of Baconian science that helped to define it as essentially Modern is its view of nature as an untamed and potentially dangerous environment that needs to be subdued and dominated by force.[10] Scientific experiments were 'ordeals' in which nature was coerced into giving up her secrets: Bacon said, 'we must put nature on the rack and compel her to bear witness'. This objectifying approach to nature was a fundamental departure from the Classical Greek and Medieval notions of nature as Providence, as a divinely provided, protective and nurturing home.

The purported linkage between science and survival proposed by Bacon and his contemporaries has had a continuing influence on the so-called hard sciences and their research aims, and on the human sciences as well. Science as a form of instrumental reason came to be treated as an insurance policy – costly, but something we can't afford to be without, given the endangering character of nature. To in any way restrain scientific enquiry or technological research and development is thus to increase, or at least fail to minimize, risk. Open-ended scientific curiosity must be actively encouraged, not just for its own sake, but because it is simply prudent to do so. Such limits as we do impose on research and experimentation are, for the most part, designed and administered by scientists themselves; the 'bioethicist' is an example. Science, we are told, needs its own ethical framework, informed by the demands of research, unencumbered by the imponderables of moral thought.

But even a casual knowledge of history of science and technology in recent times justifies the suspicion that scientific curiosity is not a morally neutral human trait. Sometimes, it may be immoral, and in need of restraint. The difficulty is in seeing which cases are which.

Take, for example, germ-line genetic manipulation, making changes in the DNA of plants, animals, and even humans, changes that will be inherited by subsequent generations and are therefore ineradicable once released into the gene pool. A common street-level criticism is that such experiments are 'playing God', and are above and beyond legitimate human curiosity, mainly because there is no way to predict all foreseeable outcomes. But this is a position based largely on instinct, and difficult to sustain outside the context of religion. Who is to say what's beyond legitimate curiosity? Who says scientists shouldn't play God, if the stakes are high enough? Who says scientists aren't in fact doing God's work?

Here is where the modern ethical 'specialist' steps in. From the perspective of a bioethicist, proper and legitimate scientific restraint on the curiosity of bioengineers, for example, might be justified by evidence that their work involves a reckless or poorly informed tampering with nature that could result in harmful, unanticipated, and possibly irreversible consequences. Framed this way, the issue can be reduced to risk management, another modern specialty. The question from this perspective is not 'Ought we to tamper?' but 'How much tampering (or "enhancement") is justified, given the predicted level of risk and the projected benefits?'

But risk management calculations would seem inadequate to the task assigned them when, as in so much of current scientific and technical endeavour, the stakes are literally incalculable. For one thing, any admission of risk will typically be weighed against promised benefits that are frequently Biblical in import: nothing less is promised by genetic researchers and engineers than the elimination of disease and, more recently, the radical extension of human life-spans – in effect, the return of humanity to its original state of Edenic perfection. On the other side of the equation, any listing of risks will, by definition, be incomplete – the essence of risk is, after all, the unknown and unexpected.

Thus, in many risk-management exercises the question comes to be posed this way: what current risk can possibly outweigh incalculable benefits such as these – benefits that are being promised not just to us, *but to all future generations*? Any Utilitarian calculation of 'the greatest good for the greatest number' will almost certainly support those whose cry is 'Full speed ahead!' And yet, tampering with the human genetic heritage seems somehow inherently wrong to many, especially when it is realized that the most passionate proponents of these technologies are speaking for corporations that stand to profit from patented techniques, and are ill-equipped to consider moral issues.

Biologist Sarah Sexton captures the issue perfectly with the wry title of an essay on human genetic engineering: 'If Cloning Is the Answer, What Was the Question?'[11] What, indeed, is the question? It might be something like, 'How can we assist nature in perfecting the human species?' But that won't do, because science does not recognize any telos or final destination in the processes of evolution – there is no 'goal' (let alone 'good' or 'bad' goals), so what could 'improvement' mean? Perfection is a value-laden term, and therefore, by their own definition, out of bounds to scientists. Nevertheless, common sense tells us that 'perfecting' humanity is an obvious motive for tinkering with human genetics.

Which leaves us no choice but to deal with this difficult adjective 'perfect'. If we are to offer a credible justification for this kind of research, we are compelled to try to understand what a more perfect human being – indeed, a more perfect human race – might be. This is quite obviously a philosophical as much as a scientific question, and so we have no choice but to elevate the discussion to the realm of moral enquiry.

In what *moral* sense, then, might germ-line genetic engineering be considered 'above and beyond' legitimate human curiosity? Clearly, the questions we need to be asking concern humanity and its goals and purposes, as opposed to technical questions about risk and benefit. Where do we draw the line between elimination of genetic defect or disease, and tweaking 'desirable' traits such as IQ or athletic ability? Without moral knowledge of this kind, how can we even know what a 'benefit' might be? Not just morality but reason also tells us that science and the technical innovations it supports cannot be carried on responsibly without parallel research into their moral implications. That research involves, inevitably, tackling at some level the oldest question in moral philosophy: what is good?

NOTES

1. *The Economist*, May 26, 2017.
2. That economy is dominated by just five corporations: Alphabet, Google's parent company, Amazon, Apple, Facebook and Microsoft – the most valuable publicly traded companies in the world.
3. Jeffrey Pfeiffer, *Dying for a Paycheck* (New York: Harper Collins, 2018).
4. John Maynard Keynes, *The General Theory of Employment and Interest* (New York: Houghton Mifflin Harcourt, 1936), 383–4.

5. John Kenneth Galbraith, *The Affluent Society* (New York: Houghton Mifflin Harcourt, 1958).

6. Thomas Hobbes, *Leviathan* (Harmondsworth: Penguin, 1982 [1651]), i. xiii. 9.

7. Francis Bacon, *Novum Organum*, Book 2 (Cambridge: Cambridge University Press, 2000 [1620]), 372.

8. And Descartes, believing that science made humans the *maîtres et possesseurs de la nature* ('masters and possessors of nature') nevertheless relied on the existence of God, a supremely perfect being, as foundational to his entire philosophic edifice.

9. Hilary Putnam, *The Collapse of the Fact/Value Dichotomy and Other Essays* (Cambridge: Harvard University Press, 2002).

10. See, Thomas More's *Utopia* (1516) for a similar perspective.

11. Sarah Sexton, "If Cloning Is the Answer, What Was the Question? Power and Decision-Making in the Geneticization of Health," *International Journal of Sustainable Development* 4, no. 4 (2001).

Chapter 2:

The Idea of Morality

1

Can universally valid moral principles be arrived at through human reason alone? For the early scientific theorists, this seemed an urgent question. There was an uneasiness in the radical rationalist movement about demolishing the foundations of Christian moral authority without providing a replacement. The French philosopher Denis Diderot (1713–84) and his Scottish contemporary David Hume (1711–76) each wrote masterworks denying the existence of God and affirming the meaninglessness of notions of vice and virtue, but both men withheld their writings from publication fearing they would be seen as apologists for wickedness. Following reason to the bitter ends, 'they found themselves [...] agreeing only in this, that Reason is incompetent to answer any fundamental question about God, or morality, or the meaning of life'.[1]

This dilemma would lead, in time, to the divorce of philosophy and science: where there had for the previous two millennia been a single knowledge-seeking vocation called 'philosophy', there would now be two separate pursuits – natural philosophy, or science, and moral philosophy, essentially a catch-all category for questions science was unequipped or unwilling to tackle. Science would limit its curiosity exclusively to 'well-posed problems', questions that can be defined clearly and precisely enough to guarantee that a 'scientific' answer can be found. All else was to be pared away. In practice this would lead to the expunging from science all references to the metaphysical, to a divine or transcendent order: the only legitimate questions were those that could be framed as 'what?' and 'how?' The question 'why?' would be largely out of bounds and consigned to philosophy as being unproductive of useful knowledge – in particular, knowledge that can be turned over to technologists for tool-making.

However, the issue of overarching goals refused to go away. So, as a substitute for the providential goals or telos prescribed for humanity in the Christian narrative, modern science substituted two important concepts: *posterity* and *progress*. The goal of scientific endeavour was to bless posterity with the results of scientific progress in the form of health, longevity, material abundance and security from the ravages of nature – that is, through progress, to leave a better world to future generations.

But moral issues cannot be evaded so easily. To pursue the question of what is meant by 'better' is to arrive inevitably in the deep woods of morality, facing the ultimate question – what is good? In the forest tangle, where paths are often indistinct and poorly marked, a compass is an asset.

2

Most of us do our best to minimize the intrusion of deep moral deliberations into our public and professional lives in the belief that, for most purposes, issues of good and bad are already taken care of by the system, and by the social and institutional rules we learn and follow throughout our lives. Besides, if we were to weigh the moral import of each and every action we perform, we'd go crazy, or at least be rendered totally unproductive.

When we do think about morality in any depth, our default position is to take the existence of good for granted.[2] Good seems real, rather than imaginary. The concept is basic to our vocabularies, in every language; we define wickedness and evil in terms of its absence. We know it when we see it, in every field of existence and experience. This confidence is remarkable, because it persists in the face of the overwhelmingly sceptical 'official' position presented to us in our secular institutions, including our schools and universities, and our corporate work environments.

Despite that confidence, though, if we're asked to *define* good most of us are stumped. We all know what a good deal is, what a good dog is, what a good holiday is. We speak fluently of good friends and neighbours, good children, and women, and men. But what about the element that these objects of admiration have in common? What is good itself?

Not only rationalist, scientific attitudes, but also an influential stream of the early twentieth-century philosophy called 'logical positivism' have supported the view that this is a foolish question; that it is not just 'poorly posed', but meaningless nonsense. It would take us too far afield to pursue logical positivism and its primary proponents (Rudolf Carnap, Carl Hempel, Ludwig Wittgenstein and others in the so-called 'Vienna Circle' of the 1920s), but its influence on both academic and popular thinking about truth and meaning was, and remains, substantial. Essentially, we are asked to believe that the only 'realities' worth thinking about are material in nature, and that science, rooted in logic and mathematics, has exclusive access to material knowledge. Thus, science is the sole arbiter for what is real and true, and all else is literal *nonsense*.

This radical viewpoint is no longer as fashionable among philosophers, or even scientists, as it once was. So perhaps, on the basis of prudence alone, it would be wise to trust our instincts on the possibility of good's existence, and consider all the possibilities.

3

Many western religious philosophers, drawing on Plato, have described good (or sometimes, *the* good, or good *itself*) as existing in a metaphysical realm beyond ordinary material reality, as a genuine, though intangible, dimension of existence. Here's the general idea: everything in the concrete and material world as we know it is merely an indistinct image of an ideal form in a higher realm of being. As a perfect realization, the ideal form embodies good. It's an idea technically called 'Platonic idealism', or Plato's theory of forms, and it has had an important influence on western philosophy and theology.

Descriptions like Plato's are evocative, beautiful, even compelling, but they are not very serviceable. The result is that the issue of good's existence has been neglected in modern moral philosophy. To correct this problem and re-incorporate the good into everyday ethical discourse, a growing number of today's moral thinkers have taken a position that does not deny the validity of idealism as a hypothesis, but tries to bring it up-to-date. What they propose is that rather than (or perhaps in addition to) existing 'beyond being', good is actually a *thing* – ineffable, perhaps, but as much a part of everyday existence as gravity. The hypothesis is that, like gravity, good exists in the world and influences events in ways that are readily observable, even though, like gravity, its precise nature remains mysterious. According to this view, good would exist even if we didn't – or as philosophers say, good is mind-independent. It has objective reality.

This perspective, if it's true, makes the consideration of good and its place in the world impossible to avoid in *any* coherent description of existence, science included. It means that in this world in which good is as much an everyday reality as gravity – in the world as we experience it as human beings – meaning and purpose are possible, even inescapable. The existence of good makes it so; it injects a goal, an endpoint, into the conversation. Aristotle stated it well:

> If there is some end of the things we do, which we desire for its own sake, clearly this must be the good. Will not knowledge of it, then, have a great influence on life? Shall we not, like archers who have a mark to aim at, be more likely to hit upon what we should? If so, we must try, in outline at least, to determine what it is.[3]

This approach to morality has a name in academia – it's called 'critical moral realism'.[4] It proposes that good is a fundamental, though ultimately indescribable, element of our reality, a mind-independent feature of the universe. The adjective 'critical' is important: it is intended to signify that the affirmation of the reality of good is something more than just a theoretical proposition, and that it is possible to test or critique its validity in much the same way as we might test a scientific hypothesis.[5]

Taken as a whole, the name 'critical moral realism' suggests that there are such things as moral *facts*, which can be verified through a process directly analogous to the one used in science, where provisional facts are tested by a formal process of replicating observations and experiments. In practice, this process amounts to an effectively unending attempt to either confirm (always provisionally) or falsify (often definitively) established fact. It's a process that has led us, in physics and astronomy, from one revolution to the another – from Ptolemy to Copernicus to Galileo to Newton to Einstein, to the quantum mechanics of the early twentieth century and beyond, into territory where today's hard-nosed physicists are unnerved by mathematical models that seem to point to something like an underlying metaphysical reality.

In science, and in moral thought, those facts which first of all seem to accurately describe reality as we experience it, and then successfully resist repeated attempts at falsification, are the ones in which we can place the most confidence. These reliable facts have achieved a broad and deep consensus within their respective fields of interest. As the philosopher Mary Midgley says: 'Facts are data – material which, for purposes of a particular enquiry, does not need to be reconsidered [...]. The word fact, in its normal usage, is indeed not properly opposed to value, but to something more like conjecture or opinion.'[6] In other words, a fact in any realm of human enquiry amounts to a discussion frozen in time, halted where a particular line of enquiry has come to a standstill, for want of further data or novel new insight.

The notion of a dichotomy between fact and value, or more accurately, between moral and scientific fact, turns out to be fictitious. Fact and value are unavoidably 'entangled', simply because human experience and endeavour, including observation and data collection and computation, is always to some greater or lesser degree value-laden. We are not robots and cannot avoid the infiltration of issues of value into everything we do, even the design of the algorithms we write to govern the actions of our machines. Nor, on the other hand, can scientific realities be excluded from thinking about values, if that thought is to have any practical application to the world we live in. Why, then, do we continue to talk about a fact/value dichotomy? Philosopher Hilary Putnam explains:

> For one thing, it is much easier to say, 'that's a value judgment', meaning, 'that's just a matter of subjective preference', than to do what Socrates tried to teach us: to examine who we are and what our deepest convictions are and hold those convictions up to the searching test of reflective examination [...]. The worst thing about the fact/value dichotomy is that in practice it functions as a discussion-stopper, and not just a discussion-stopper, but a thought-stopper.[7]

From the perspective of critical moral realism, basic value judgements such as 'genocide is wrong' cannot be both true and false. They are either true (or false) for reasons offered, or for reasons not yet fully uncovered. For the moral realist, ethical claims are similar to statements like 'the sky is blue'. They can be verified by real-world observation and experience, and demonstrated to be true or false. That is, they meet the same criteria of *fact* as material facts do. Assertions that slavery is defensible, or the handicapped ought to be destroyed at birth, or that adulterers ought to be stoned to death, or that animals have no right to humane treatment, are quite as false as the statement that water flows uphill. Their falsity is not just a matter of somebody's opinion: it's a fact.

It is worth pointing out, parenthetically, that no fact in modern scientific consensus is more than about 450 years old, while consensus on moral issues can and often does stretch back to the beginnings of recorded history. It is also noteworthy that when shifts in moral consensus occur – when slavery is abolished, or torture is outlawed, or the right of animals to humane treatment is recognized, or women's suffrage is enacted – they tend to have a much more significant impact on daily life than even a genuine scientific revolution like the displacement of Newton's physics by Einstein's relativity.

4

The claim, then, is that both moral and scientific facts are established by consensus, and the broader and deeper and longer-lasting that consensus is, the more confidence we can have in the associated body of knowledge. When a significant shift in that consensus occurs, we do not expect to go back to earlier views, especially where moral knowledge is concerned. At the same time, however, the possibility of falsification is never completely extinguished.

The truth or falsity of a statement, either moral or scientific, does not depend on how well it fits with some theoretical, a priori assumption that must be accepted on faith – though these may well lurk in the background, for instance as a belief in the real existence of good, or in the ability of reason to see deep into nature's workings. The truth and reliability of these statements of fact depends, instead, on a network of prior knowledge linking the statement we want to verify with others of the same kind that have their own network of evidence, and ultimately to 'the whole map of our experience and of the world which we believe to surround us'.[8]

And so, in the end, the body of fact that makes up our total understanding of the world is like a vast crossword puzzle, in which having the correct answer to the clue for 1 Down may depend on knowing the correct answer to 3 Across, and so on until the puzzle is complete. Reality, though, is for all practical purposes infinite, and so the puzzle is never done. And as long as that's the case it is always possible that an incorrect answer will be discovered deep in the matrix, forcing reconsideration of every other related answer, in principle up to and including the whole puzzle.

Finally, Hilary Putnam makes a salient point in arguing for the factual nature of moral knowledge, via the pragmatist philosopher John Dewey:

> If it is possible to do science without supposing that one needs a metaphysical foundation for the enterprise, it is equally possible to live an ethical life without supposing that one needs a metaphysical foundation. [...] As John Dewey urged long ago, the objectivity that ethical claims require is not the kind that is provided by a Platonic or other foundation that is

there in advance of our engaging in ethical life and ethical reflection; it is the ability to withstand the sort of criticism that arises in the problematic situations that we actually encounter [...].[9]

If the moral realists are correct, as I believe they are, then it is crucial that moral fact be integrated into the formal matrix of knowledge so that the two kinds of fact – both tested sources of knowledge – can be made explicitly supportive of one another, cresting a more robust and resilient structure, one that is less likely to conceal catastrophic flaws, one that reliably reflects reality in all its complexity.[10]

NOTES

1. Carl L. Becker, *The Heavenly City of the Eighteenth-Century Philosophers* (New Haven: Yale University Press, 1932), 82.

2. My use of the terms 'ethics' and 'morality' herein follow the widely accepted distinction in moral realism: *morality* deals with the common-sense assessments and behaviours of everyday living and *ethics* with the theoretical constructs that shape morality.

3. Aristotle, *Nicomachean Ethics*, Book 1:2 (ca. 325 BCE).

4. Some of the better known adherents and proponents include Hannah Arendt, Theodor Adorno, Erich Fromm, Herbert Marcuse, Walter Benjamin, Jurgen Habermas, Bernard Lonergan, Terry Eagleton, Mary Midgley, Hilary Putnam, Zygmunt Bauman, Ian Barbour and Michael Polanyi.

5. The distinction between realism and idealism is central to philosophy and is discussed in most introductory texts. Jacques Maritain was among the first to use the 'critical' distinction in connection with realism in *Degrees of Knowledge*, trans. Gerald B. Phelan (Notre Dame: Notre Dame University Press, 1995); and *A Preface to Metaphysics* (Salem, NH: Ayer Company Publishers, 1987).

6. Mary Midgley, *Wisdom, Information and Wonder* (London: Routledge, 2001), 156.

7. Putnam, *The Collapse of the Fact/Value Dichotomy and Other Essays*, 42.

8. Midgley, *Wisdom, Information and Wonder*, 137.

9. Putnam, *The Collapse of the Fact/Value Dichotomy and Other Essays*, 94.

10. An excellent, and authoritative, detailing of this approach to epistemology can be found in Susan Haack, *Evidence and Inquiry: Towards Reconstruction in Epistemology* (Oxford: Blackwell, 1995).

Chapter 3:

Biology and Good

1

To accept that good is part of the primordial order of things, folded in, like gravity, is to accept that humanity must in some way be aligned with or touched by good; that good is implicated in our make-up and constitution. How could it be otherwise? Just as we are susceptible to gravity and other natural phenomena, we must in some sense be influenced by good, and shaped by it, just as physical objects in space cannot avoid the influence of gravity.[1]

Certainly, we are able to sense good and to know it when we see it. We have various names for this ability: conscience, or moral sense, or our moral compass, or the moral impulse within us. Biologist Marc Hauser concludes in his landmark study, *Moral Minds*:

> We are endowed with a moral acquisition device. Infants are born with the building blocks for making sense of the causes and consequences of actions, and their early capacities grow and interface with others to generate moral judgments. Infants are also equipped with a suite of unconscious, automatic emotions that can reinforce the expression of some actions while blocking others. Together, these capacities enable children to build moral systems.[2]

Aristotle said something very similar of the moral sense: 'Neither by nature, then, nor contrary to nature do the virtues arise in us; rather we are adapted by nature to receive them, and are made perfect by habit'.[3] Eight hundred years later St. Augustine was grappling with the mysteries of this faculty when he concluded that morality is the product of charity, which is the *pondus* – the gravitational force – of love that attracts us to 'that which we ought to love'. Immanuel Kant in the eighteenth century confessed to being awed by two things: 'the starry heavens above me and the mystery of the moral law within me'. Philosophers Noam Chomsky and John Rawls speak, in our own times, of our innate moral grammar.

This simple thought experiment may be helpful:

Fact: we are, like everything else in the universe, products of the Big Bang. We are composed of the same basic materials as the stars.

Consider: you are at home reading a book; you feel thirsty. You get up and pour yourself a glass of water and drink it. The water drains into your stomach, and from there seeps into your bloodstream, into cells, eventually reaching your brain. There, *the water begins to think*.[4]

Are we the universe thinking? Put more broadly, is consciousness itself an inherently moral phenomenon, as Aristotle and Augustine suggest? Is consciousness in some sense oriented towards the good?

2

Hobbes saw human beings in their natural state as innately savage and brutishly self-interested, the self, or consciousness, being focused on its own preservation. He said we were able to build stable communities only when war-weariness and fear for our personal security led us to consent to domination by an absolute ruler. The evidence presented above suggests something very different: it is not terror but our innate moral sensibility that spurs us to look for ways to make our world a better, more just and convivial place. We do this by building those social, political, legal and economic institutions that define any civilization.

As the sociologist Zygmunt Bauman says:

[M]oral responsibility [...] is the first reality of the self, a starting point rather than a product of society. It precedes all engagement with the Other, be it through knowledge, evaluation, suffering or doing. It has therefore no 'foundation' – no cause, no determining factor. [...] there is no self before the moral self, morality being the ultimate, non-determined presence, indeed an act of creation *ex nihilo*, if ever there was one.[5]

The idea is by now familiar: morality, the human expression of good, is a reflection of the numinous order of things.

As is the case with gravity, or time, or consciousness, those other everyday imponderables that we can identify but not explain, we do not need to understand the origin and genealogy of good in order to study it profitably. We can accept it as an indisputable phenomenon of which we are aware through both observation (i.e. through our senses) and through intuition and introspection. In other words, it is part of what is sometimes called the 'phenomenological world': the world that precedes formal, organized knowledge; the world to which such knowledge addresses itself.[6]

Good can be studied philosophically as a concept, but it can also be studied in a traditionally 'scientific' way. As the scientist does, the moral inquirer will begin with a conjecture or a hypothesis, and go on to propose formal experiments and organized observations, the purpose of which is to challenge the hypothesis by testing it against the phenomenological evidence. Those conjectures are most reliable and secure, which successfully, in repeated tests, remain unfalsified and therefore viable, and in that sense factual or true.

The hypothesis of an innate moral grammar is one such success story. Psychologist Steven Pinker writes that, in his science's tentative exploration of the 'new' territory of morality and the moral sense now widely conceded to exist, 'moral intuitions are being drawn out of people in the lab, on websites and in brain scanners, and are being explained with tools from game theory, neuroscience and evolutionary biology'. The result, he says, has been that 'the human moral sense turns out to be an organ of considerable complexity, with quirks that reflect its evolutionary history and its neurobiological foundations'.[7]

For example, psychologists have established that an individual's moral reactions to a given situation are typically immediate and powerful, but people frequently have trouble explaining why they responded in the way they did. Psychologist Jonathan Haidt has concluded that when it comes to their lives as moral agents, people generally do not think moral problems through in a logical way, but rather provide after-the-fact rationalizations for conclusions that seem to be arrived at unconsciously, intuitively or instinctively.[8]

In the continuing search for biological causes of moral behaviour the cognitive neuroscientist Joshua Greene and colleagues at Princeton University have watched blood flow functions on MRI brain scanners as subjects are asked to respond to various moral dilemmas presented to them.[9] The experimenters have established that areas of the brain known to be involved in emotional responses are invariably among the regions active in moral decision-making: where those emotion-related regions of the brain have been damaged, subjects are apt to make decisions on strictly utilitarian grounds. So that, for example, they will see no dilemma in whether a surgeon should or should not kill a comatose but otherwise healthy patient in order to harvest her organs to save one or more dying patients whose achievements and future potential for doing good in the world are unimpeachable. For them, the simple utilitarian numbers make the decision an obvious one.

What do we learn about morality from this biological research? Not much. The brain states measured by the scientist represent the *conditions* for whatever thought is going on in the subject. The thought itself is quite another thing, so that what the neurologist knows while observing her instruments and what the subject knows while thinking are fundamentally distinct from one another. Brain-scan experiments like these are classic reductionist science. While they may inform us that emotion is involved in making moral judgements, they tell us nothing about morality itself. The fact that the brain responds in specific and identifiable ways to moral challenges merely raises the question of whether electro-chemical brain states determine thought, or vice versa. Most scientists prefer to think the former, of course, because this allows them to conduct experiments and collect numerical data. But this seems to be an unjustifiable position. After all, the entire premise of psychotherapy and related 'talk-therapy' disciplines is that thought can alter brain states – indeed, there is much evidence that thought can alter physiology throughout the body, as is demonstrated most dramatically in yogic disciplines.

3

It would seem clear, according to the best evidence available to us, both moral and scientific, that we can safely assign the existence of an innate moral sensibility in human beings to the 'fact' column. The fabled 'moral compass' exists. What, then, of that other issue raised by Hobbes and his rationalist friends, the essentially selfish essence of human nature? It is an assumption worth examining because, as we'll see later, it is accepted as a truism in economics and other social sciences. The question is, are humans essentially (though perhaps not exclusively) self-interested, or are we essentially (though perhaps not exclusively) other-directed, or altruistic? 'Essentially' here should be understood in the sense of what is fundamental to our nature, a defining characteristic of our makeup.

Evolutionary biology has lately attempted to make room for enquiry into the nature of morality within this characteristically reductionist discipline. It has done this by attempting to show that even though Darwin's model of natural selection through competition for scarce resources clearly operates on the basis of self-interest (what is best for the organism), it is still possible for an individual organism such as a human being to behave in ways that are authentically altruistic, or other-directed. That is, in ways in which no payback, hidden or explicit, is expected or involved.

Darwin himself found the presence of morality in humans difficult to understand, given our evolution from a 'hairy, tailed quadruped'. In a long chapter devoted to the topic in *The Descent of Man* (1871) he argued that our innate other-directedness is an evolutionary trait common to social creatures. This trait, he believed, evolved in two stages: first through the need to nurture young in birds, and then in mammals (the neglected young do not survive to procreate); and second, as humans gain intellectual capacity they are able to reflect on their own past behaviour and that of others, and form judgements based on the results. This, he believed, led to the development of conscience, 'the supreme judge and monitor' of behaviour.

A modern sociobiologist might describe the process like this: natural selection leads to the dominance of organisms that favour tit-for-tat behaviour, because it serves their survival interests better than pure selfishness. 'You scratch my back and I'll scratch yours' is sound survival strategy, and, indeed, is widely practised even among non-human animals.[10] This is what is called 'reciprocal altruism', and it needs to be distinguished from true altruism in which there is no expectation of reward, or to put in another way, in which a cost is incurred but no benefit expected in return.

A growing number of anthropologists and economists have accepted a modified version of the theory of reciprocal altruism as a description of a uniquely human evolutionary adaptation, refining it slightly as 'strong reciprocity'. This is described as a tendency within groups for individuals to cooperate with others, and seek out and punish those who don't follow the rules of cooperation. Although strong reciprocity is not overtly selfish, it is strategic. The intent of the punishment is not to convert, but to drive the cheaters out; successful adaptation means 'focusing our cooperative efforts on those who are trustworthy'.[11]

As ingenious as this theory of the biological origins of moral behaviour may be – and regardless of whether it seems even remotely plausible – it still has nothing whatever to say about the nature of morality itself. Transferred to the human realm it leaves fundamental questions unanswered, for example: what is it that makes cheating immoral (and not just bad strategy)? Morality cannot simply be a matter of survival technique; one can imagine any number of circumstances in which good survival strategy is also immoral – such as stealing a child's life jacket to keep oneself afloat in a shipwreck. Or, why do we honour the individual who sacrifices himself for the child by doing the opposite? In the real world we all inhabit, self-sacrifice without recompense is a feature of behaviour we see routinely, and consider to be highly virtuous. Evolutionary theory brings us no closer to answering Socrates' question: What is good? What is virtuous conduct?

Evolutionary biology, neurobiology, cognitive neuroscience, psychology and all the other sciences that deal with the brain and cognition can and do describe brain activity that is associated with thought, and speculate imaginatively and even usefully about behaviour and how it may be encoded into organisms, through eons of natural selection, as successful survival traits. Neither individually nor collectively, however, do these sciences provide an escape from the need to deal with the basic essence of morality, the metaphysical question of good.

4

Early in the history of moral philosophy Plato poses a question that is directly relevant to issues of biological necessity and human behaviour. It appears in a dialogue between Socrates and a man named Euthyphro, and so is remembered as the Euthyphro Dilemma. The two are discussing the nature of piety, of reverence for the gods. Socrates asks: is something good because it is favoured by the gods, or does the fact the gods look upon something favourably *make* it good? In terms of modern religious debate, the question becomes one of crucial significance with respect to the idea that God's will is the foundation of ethics, that God determines what is good and what is not. This is known as divine command theory. (How one comes to know God's will is a complicating issue that we need not deal with here: generally, it is through divinely inspired texts, testimony of the saintly, or through prayer.) The Euthyphro Dilemma challenges divine command theory by asking whether morally good acts are morally good because they are acts that have been willed by God, or does God will the acts because they are morally good? Problems arise either way.

If whatever God wills must be, by definition, morally good, then the question of what is moral is emptied of meaning, becoming tautological: how do we know an action is good? Because God wills it. Why does God will it? Because it is good. This leaves the aspiring human with little to cling to by way of practical guidance. To escape the tautology, it would be necessary to imagine God calling on some prior, external notion of morality, an idea which, in religious terms, is nonsensical.

Brought further up to date, into the realms of sociobiology and evolutionary biology and biological explanations for altruism, the same kinds of objections apply – the Euthyphro Dilemma remains. Plainly stated: can any biologically ordained preference whatsoever justify a claim of moral or immoral behaviour? If science were to discover a gene for racism, should we then be forgiven for becoming racists? The answer has to be: of course not. Where does 'of course not' come from? It can't be biologically determined, because that would mean we are biologically determined to be both racist and not-racist, which is nonsense. So the moral judgement behind 'of course not' must be rooted elsewhere.

To close the circle, looking for an explanation of altruistic, other-directed, selfless behaviour in some biological circumstance or condition makes no sense, because morality exists *outside* biology. We are left no further ahead than poor Diderot, who strove with his rationalist colleagues to 'know more than [theologians] do', and to 'show them that we are better, and that philosophy makes more good men than sufficient or efficacious grace',[12] but who was fatally handicapped in this ambition by his prior conclusion that 'the original source of things has no more regard to good above ill than to hot above cold'.[13]

There is more than a whiff of deliberate, even amusing, self-deception in the biologist's approach to moral issues, nicely illustrated in this apocryphal anecdote:

> It's late at night, a man is searching for something on hands and knees under a streetlight, and a passerby asks what he has lost. 'My car keys', the man answers. 'I dropped them somewhere in the ditch across the road'.

> 'Then why', asks the passerby, 'are you searching here?'

> 'Because the light's better', comes the reply.

NOTES

1. Time is another aspect of our existence that, in Einsteinian science, has no concrete existence, though the experience and its vagaries are central to our everyday life. See Chap. 10.
2. Marc Hauser, *Moral Minds: The Nature of Right and Wrong* (New York: Harper Perennial, 2006), 303.
3. Aristotle, *Nicomachean Ethics,* Book 2:1, 1003a.
4. I have borrowed this illustration from California physicist and cosmologist Brian Swimme.
5. Zygmunt Bauman, *Postmodern Ethics* (Oxford: Blackwell, 1993), 13.
6. There is an obvious, and fascinating, relationship here with the philosopher Henri Bergson's *élan vital* in the material world and time as *duration*, the complexities of which are beyond the scope of this book. See Chap. 10.
7. Steven Pinker, "The Moral Instinct," *New York Times*, January 13, 2008.
8. Pinker, "The Moral Instinct."
9. Laura Helmuth, "Emotions Are Rationale for Some Moral Dilemmas," *Science*, September 2001.
10. Robert Trivers, "The Evolution of Reciprocal Altruism," *Quarterly Review of Biology* 46 (1971): 35–57.
11. Hauser, *Moral Minds.*
12. Denis Diderot, *Ouevres* (1875–77), II, 345.
13. Diderot, *Ouevres*, XIX, 464.

Chapter 4:

The Alchemy of Capitalism

1

The idea that good has no real existence outside religion, superstition and the conventions of human language is arguably the reigning viewpoint within the social sciences today. It's an idea whose most vocal early advocate was a contemporary of Thomas Hobbes, Francis Bacon and René Descartes – the philosopher Baruch Spinoza (1632–77). Like his fellow rationalists, Spinoza did not deny the existence of God, rather he identified God with nature, using the terms interchangeably. His naturalized God had no goals or desires, and so ethics could not be a product of divine will. Spinoza's viewpoint became scandalously famous: 'Nothing happens in nature', he asserted, 'which might be attributed to any defect in it'. That is, the world as we find it is perfection, and everything that happens in nature fulfils a necessary purpose. That being the case, he reasoned, it is a sign of ignorance to describe some actions as good and others wicked: the only appropriate definition of good, he said, is simply 'that which we certainly know to be useful to us'. [1]

Spinoza was of the view that, using the newly worked-out processes of scientific enquiry, the purposes of each of the human 'passions' (we would say drives or emotions) would soon be deciphered, and understanding human relationships would then be no more challenging than calculating the motions of the planets. The proper, rational, attitude to so-called human vices – lust, gluttony, greed and so on – was not to condemn them, he said, but to learn their purpose, because they certainly *had* a purpose in the over-all scheme of things.

As shocking as it seemed at the time, Spinoza's radical view of good as 'that which is certainly useful to us' was to be incorporated into a powerful new ideology that was emerging in Europe. We call it, looking back, liberal capitalism, and it was evolving within the social and intellectual stew that included such ingredients as the Scientific Revolution, the rise of the Protestantism of Luther and Calvin, increased international trade, the opening of the New World, urbanization, the reform of medieval farming practices, and other trends that help define early Modernism. This new ideology located the source of human well-being in economic behaviour, as dictated by the competitive dynamics of the market economy. It would quickly become a fertile field of study which, as Spinoza had urged, addressed prominent human vices – self-interest, competitiveness, envy, greed – in terms of their utility in business and commerce.

One prominent theorizer was Pierre Nicole (1625–95), whose tract *Of Charity and Self-Love* (1675) ruminated on the mechanics of the capitalist market, noting that:

> by the means and help of [...] commerce all necessaries for this life are supplied without intermixing charity [i.e., love of others] with it. So that in states where charity has no admittance, because true religion is banished there, men do not cease to live with as much peace, safety, and comfort, as if they lived in a Republic of Saints.

For Nicole, the market, though not a replacement for 'true' morality, was an alternative and highly satisfactory way of producing the conditions for happiness through the enlightened management of self-interest.

Thus, it is as a *moral science* that economics first takes centre stage in rationalist thought.[2] In Bernard de Mandeville's widely read epic poem, 'Fable of the Bees' (1714), we learn that the 'purpose' of self-interested vice in the form of avarice, pride and vanity is to fuel economic activity and wealth production. In his fable, life in the hive had always been idyllic, with every individual's wants and desires served by industrious, entrepreneurial, bees, most of whom were unabashedly unscrupulous in their business affairs. But there arose complaints about the cheating and fraud, the loudest of which, ironically, came from the worst of the offenders. The god of the hive, Jove, became disgusted and angrily evicted the miscreants. The economy of the hive promptly collapsed and the remaining bees were reduced to misery because, being virtuous individuals, they were not very industrious, and were no longer driven to compete with one another.

In a commentary appended to his poem Mandeville wrote:

> [W]hat we call evil in this world, moral as well as natural, is the grand
> principle that makes us sociable creatures, the solid basis, the life and
> support of all trades and employments without exception: [...] there we
> must look for the true origin of all Arts and Sciences.

Wickedness, in other words, was actually a precursor and helpmate to good.

Despite its antisocial overtones, Mandeville's fable and subsequent writings by others on the same theme were deeply influential among the early
theorizers of emerging liberal capitalism. In relatively short order the idea
of a market economy in which prosperity is driven by intense, self-interested
competition would push aside the medieval idea of commercial activity as a
necessary evil, one that needed to be kept under strict control. For a thousand years and more the moral teachings of the Catholic Church had treated
wealth-producing economic activity as a moral hazard. It interfered with the
real business of life, which was to follow virtue, strive for self-knowledge
and seek salvation. Where participation in business and commerce were
unavoidable, the rules of morality were to be followed just as in all other
aspects of life.

Self-interest and avarice were passions that needed careful repression. As
R.H. Tawney writes in his classic *Religion and the Rise of Capitalism*:

> There is no place in medieval theory for economic activity which is not
> related to moral ends, and to found a science of society upon the assump-
> tion that the appetite for economic gain is a constant and measurable force,
> to be accepted, like other natural forces, as an inevitable and self-evident
> *datum*, would have appeared to the medieval thinker as hardly less irra-
> tional or less immoral than to make the premise of social philosophy the
> unrestrained operation of such necessary human attributes as pugnacity
> or the sexual instinct.[3]

But this is precisely what the rationalist ideology of Hobbes, Spinoza,
Mandeville and their contemporaries would accomplish – the founding of
a science of society based upon competition, self-interest and appetite for
material gain. Voltaire (1694–1778), as one of the ideology's leading expo-
nents, was thus the conservative medieval moralists' worst nightmare. It

was a role the writer, playwright, and poet revelled in with ribald glee as he penned his novel *Candide*, the virtuous hero of which finds his moral scruples do not serve him well in a world made in the image of rationalist economic theory.

For Enlightenment thinkers, self-interest was what made the world go around, and since, as Spinoza had affirmed, good is 'that which we certainly know to be useful to us', self-interest could only be good. For Voltaire, self-interest was 'the foundation of commerce, the eternal link between men'. While God was clearly capable of 'creating beings solely concerned with the good of others [...] [He] has ordained things differently. Let us not condemn the instinct He has given us, and let us put it to the use He commands'.[4] Here, with the precision of a great writer, he has encapsulated the heart and soul of Enlightenment thought as it is found in the ideology of liberal market capitalism.

The idea that the amenities and satisfactions of civilization are really a product of vice, and that in order for good to flourish we must encourage what is worst rather than best in humanity is, on the face of it, perverse. It would take a thinker of the stature of Adam Smith (1723–90) to make sense of it in a way we continue to accept to this day.

2

Adam Smith was a moral philosopher of strong rationalist leanings, a product of the Scottish Enlightenment that flowered in eighteenth-century Glasgow and Edinburgh. He published his masterwork, *The Wealth of Nations* (1776), two years after Voltaire's death, and a century after Spinoza had flourished. It was the same year in which the British colonies in North America famously asserted their independence from Great Britain, with a historic Declaration redolent of rationalist ideas in its references to 'self-evident' truths, and 'Laws of Nature'.

The founder of modern economic theory, Smith set out the basic premises of today's mainstream economic theory in his great treatise, in which the role of self-interest in creating public welfare is worked out in consummate detail. He began from what he took to be an obvious and inarguable axiom:

> [M]an has almost constant occasion for the help of his brethren, and it is in vain for him to expect it from their benevolence only. He will be more

likely to prevail if he can interest their self-love in his favour, and show them that it is for their own advantage to do for him what he requires of them [...]. It is not through the benevolence of the butcher, the brewer or the baker that we expect our dinner, but from their regard to their own interests. We address ourselves, not to their humanity but to their self-love, and never talk to them of our own necessities but of their advantages. Nobody but a beggar chooses to depend chiefly upon the benevolence of his fellow citizens.[5]

It is important to note how Smith frames as objective reality what is in fact his own, highly subjective, perspective on the world around him, a recurring feature of rationalist Enlightenment-era thought going all the way back to Hobbes and his dystopic imaginings of primitive humanity. To take one example, the 'beggars' Smith refers in the quotation above were, of course, a prominent reality of his world of emergent market capitalism. Then, as now, they were the collateral damage of economic expansion and the inequitable sharing of burgeoning wealth. But then, as now, few among this dispossessed class 'chose' to be beggars.

Despite the inevitable influence of his day-to-day observations, Smith did not model his grand economic design on the evidence (which was not being collected in any systematic way) but built it instead on his a priori, theoretical beliefs. He had in fact arrived at his conclusions about the self-regulating nature of the market long before he wrote his landmark treatise, *The Wealth of Nations* (1776). It is in his *Theory of Moral Sentiments* (1759) that the iconic notion of an 'invisible hand' at work behind the scenes in capitalist markets first makes its appearance. The context was a discussion of the single-minded pursuit of profit and the lust for luxury goods among wealthy mill owners, character traits that incidentally gave life-sustaining jobs to impoverished workers. Smith wrote, '[The greedy mill owners] are led by an invisible hand to [...] without intending it, without knowing it, advance the interest of society. [...] We take pleasure in beholding the perfection of so beautiful and grand a system'.

To be sure, Smith had a nuanced view of the human vices compared to many of his followers, and he was no fan of greed and avarice, especially among the ruling classes. 'All for ourselves, and nothing for other people, seems, in every age of the world, to have been the vile maxim of the masters of mankind'. Egoism, or self-interest, was the abiding passion of all people, he said, but the ruling classes were in the fortunate position of being able to freely indulge their greed. 'They are themselves always, and without any exception, the greatest spendthrifts in the society'.[6] In defining human nature as essentially self-interested and greedy, Smith also recognized that there is a side to human nature that can be generous and sympathetic. This he credited to a feature of human psychology that he described as an in-built, impartial observer in each of us, a faculty similar to what most of us call conscience, or perhaps, a moral compass.

But this moral faculty, he believed, was not nearly as effective in guiding human behaviour as the economic relations that govern our lives as producers and consumers, landlords and merchants, manufacturers, farmers, labourers and craftspeople. The dynamics of the capitalist market economy, Smith believed, were a form of natural law, discovered rather than invented. In retrospect, of course, we are able to see that the rules and conventions of economic intercourse that emerged with the market capitalism of Smith's time are human inventions, frequently imposed through edict and the force of arms. Smith, however, saw in them God's benevolent hand guiding the affairs of humanity. In transactions of the marketplace the individual person

> intends only his own gain, and he is *in this, as in many other cases, led by an invisible hand* to promote an end which was no part of his intention. Nor is it always the worse for the society that it was no part of it. By pursuing his own interest he frequently promotes that of the society more effectually than when he really intends to promote it. I have never known much good done by those who affected to trade for the public good. It is an affection indeed, not very common among merchants, and very few words need to be employed in dissuading them from it.[7]

Smith's Newton-like formalization of contemporary economic practice was among the loftiest products of the exhilarating intellectual atmosphere of the early Modern era, in which nothing seemed beyond rational, scientific explanation; no mystery insoluble, no problem immune to human understanding and resolution.[8]

When fused with the radical ideas of a new philosophy called Utilitarianism it would become the foundation upon which subsequent market theory has been built.

3

Spinoza's shocking notion that good is simply 'that which is certainly useful to us' was central to Utilitarianism, which advocated a forthright, reductionist approach to morality and moral decision-making. For proponents Jeremy Bentham (1743–1832) and John Stuart Mill (1806–73), the lives of humans, for all their apparent complexity, boil down to the pursuit of pleasure and the avoidance of pain. Self-interest is king; '[h]uman beings', said Bentham, 'are deficient in altruism'.[9] Based on these purely theoretical assumptions, the two concocted a moral philosophy which famously concludes that those actions are *good* which create the greatest balance of pleasure over pain for the greatest number.[10] Mill, in particular, made serious efforts to list various pleasures in ranking order, and even to assign numerical values to them, so that ethical problems might be solved by arithmetic, and social institutions engineered around algorithms. Inevitably, elements of Utilitarianism became embedded in the economic thought that was brewing in the minds of cutting-edge thinkers of the time who often considered themselves both economists and moral philosophers.

Because people were 'deficient in altruism' and tended to think of work as a disutility – '*Aversion*, not *desire*, is the only emotion which labour, taken by itself, is qualified to produce', Bentham wrote[11] – Utilitarians concluded that the only way to advance the cause of civility and prosperity in society was through systematic, structural coercion. This was to be applied humanely, by social institutions engineered to channel 'natural' anti-social impulses into communal welfare. Chief among these institutions was the capitalist market economy, which rewarded self-interested behaviour while at the same time producing communal well-being. Age-old English social welfare measures financed by local councils and churches were actively discouraged by the Utilitarians as providing an incentive to laziness. The key to dealing rationally with the indolent was to inflict pain upon them in excess of the pleasure they derived from their idleness. The poor house and debtor's prisons of Dickensian fame resulted.

Some insight into the role institutions were to play in the Utilitarians' mechanistic world may be had from one of Jeremy Bentham's cleverest inventions – the Panopticon prison.[12] Pitched to the British government as a money-saving way to incarcerate criminals, Bentham's design was for a cylindrical building of six stories with a slim central tower in the middle of a large interior courtyard. The doughnut-shaped, outer cylindrical structure would be divided into hundreds of individual pie-shaped cells, each with a window on the outside wall, and a door of steel bars facing into the courtyard with its tower. Seen from above, it had the appearance of a wheel with a hub, but no spokes. The courtyard observation hub was carefully designed (with Venetian blinds, among other features) so that inmates would be unable to see whether or not it was occupied by guards at any given moment.

In this way, prisoners would be isolated from one another, and potentially, at least, under constant surveillance from the watch tower. But, Bentham argued, *actual* constant surveillance would be unnecessary, because prisoners would have to assume they were being watched, and behave accordingly. The very design of the building, he said, would ensure that prisoners would behave as if they were being watched. Bentham described the Panopticon as 'a new mode of obtaining power of mind over mind, in a quantity hitherto without example'.[13] A handful of the prisons were built to Bentham's specifications, the best surviving examples of which are on Cuba's Isla de la Juventud, where a group of these buildings, long disused, has been converted to a museum and tourist attraction.

4

The Utilitarian approach of thinking about society and its ills is by no means a mere relic of the past.[14] Privacy advocates have long expressed the fear that a Panopticon effect is being created by the proliferation of CCTV cameras in urban environments. London, at this writing, had about 500,000, and in the 'special economic zone' of Shenzhen city in China, authorities are in the process of installing a projected total of two million surveillance cameras, networked and backed up by American face-recognition technology. (New York City, by contrast, has fewer than 20,000.)

Another example of contemporary adaptation of the technique is the widely used enterprise resource planning (ERP) software that allows continuous, keystroke-by-keystroke monitoring of workers employed in telecom-based jobs such as telemarketing and customer service. Vendors of the software emphasize the self-surveillance aspect in their marketing materials. Through ERP, service industries become virtual assembly lines, subject to all the speed-up efficiencies that characterized the Taylorism time-and-motion management of the early-twentieth-century workplace so heartily despised by workers themselves. Currently, the global market for ERP software is estimated to be more than US $80 billion.

And, of course there are the Internet applications grouped together as 'social media', which offer, at no charge, the ability to keep in touch with friends, family and acquaintances, and whose business plans all centre on collection of users' personal information for sale to advertisers and others, including political operatives. Millions of users around the world have been slow to realize that, as the old saw warns, 'if the service is free, then you are the product'.

Google's parent company, Alphabet, has a subsidiary called Sidewalk Labs, which specializes in upgrading existing urban centres using the kinds of surveillance and data collection we've become familiar with on the Internet. Big data would be used to regulate everything from traffic flows to water and electricity consumption and much more. Other data-centric Silicon Valley companies are exploring urban development up to and including the design of entire new cities. For better or worse, the rationalist project of re-engineering of the human condition continues apace.

Bentham's Panopticon sought a humane, efficient way to impose discipline in prisons, but in doing so it reduced inmates to the condition of lab rats, with little or no consideration given to the psychological impact of near-complete isolation combined with an absolute lack of privacy, day and night. (Bentham commented that the isolation might provide prisoners with the opportunity to reflect on their crimes, though this seems to have been an afterthought.) In this as in other Utilitarian social schemes the human being is treated as a component of a larger, machine-like *system*, susceptible to well-engineered manipulations of his or her environment, whether social, institutional or physical. The goal of Utilitarian social policy, in short, was to induce a kind of synthetic moral behaviour among men and women, *in spite of themselves*, through the rational design of institutions. It fits seamlessly with Smith's self-regulating market. The system, as it would continue to evolve in all its mechanistic efficiency, is one that does not encourage considered choice among its human components, but rather promotes a docile compliance with the 'rational' dictates of technology and machine-like social and economic arrangements, reifying reason in algorithms.

NOTES

1. Baruch Spinoza, *Ethica* (1677).
2. See Bernard Hodgson's *Economics as Moral Science* (New York: Springer-Verlag, 2001) for a comprehensive discussion.
3. R. H. Tawney, *Religion and the Rise of Capitalism* (New York: Harcourt, Brace and Company, 1926).
4. Voltaire, *Lettres Philosophique (Letters on the English)* (1734).
5. Adam Smith, *An Inquiry into the Nature and Causes of The Wealth of Nations* (Digireads.com ebook, 2009), 12. The extract is preceded by this less famous, but revealing passage:

> Nobody ever saw a dog make a fair and deliberate exchange of one bone for another with another dog [...]. When an animal wants to obtain something either of a man or of another animal, it has no other means of persuasion but to gain the favour of those whose service it requires. Man sometimes uses the same arts with his brethren, and when he has no other means of engaging them to act according to his inclinations, endeavours by every servile and fawning attention to obtain their good will. He has not time, however, to do this upon every occasion. In civilized society he stands at all times in need of the cooperation and assistance of great multitudes, while his whole life is scarce sufficient to gain the friendship of a few persons [...].

6. Smith, *The Wealth of Nations*, Book II, chap. III, 346, para. 36.
7. Smith, *The Wealth of Nations*, 264. Emphasis added.
8. Another highlight is the work of Smith's contemporary, the French political philosopher Claude Henri Saint-Simon (1769–1825). He saw a future in which politics would be replaced by scientifically engineered institutions for 'transforming human irrationalities into rational behaviour', much as the capitalist market of Smith transformed individual vice into collective well-being. Governance would be reduced to administration, to be undertaken by industrial leaders and scientists. His ideas for a technical meritocracy found favour, especially, with a new class of scientifically knowledgeable craftsmen and technicians spawned by rampant industrialism: they called themselves engineers, a group still known for its hard-nosed, positivist world-view. The pioneering sociologist, August Comte (1798–1857) brought similar ultra-rationalist expectations to his nascent field of study (he had for a time served as Saint-Simon's secretary), believing that social intercourse must be governed by invariable natural laws; he

called his sociology 'social physics'. His was an early expression of a soon-to-be universal 'physics envy' among social scientists – the desire to place fields of study such as economics, sociology, anthropology and psychology on the firm, mathematics-based footings of natural law as immutable and predictable as chemistry and hydraulics.

9. W. Stark, ed., *Jeremy Bentham's Economic Writings* (New York: Burr Franklin. Vol. I, 1952; Vols. II, III, 1954), 427–28.

10. John Stuart Mill, *Utilitarianism* (1861).

11. Stark, *Jeremy Bentham's Economic Writings*, 214.

12. Jeremy Bentham, *Proposal for a New and Less Expensive Mode of Employing and Reforming Convicts* (London, 1798).

13. Jeremy Bentham, *The Panopticon Writings*, ed. Miran Bozovic (London: Verso, 1995), 29–95.

14. Interest in the Panopticon prison was revived by the French philosopher Michel Foucault's study of 'disciplinary' society and its use of various forms of surveillance to encourage conformity to accepted norms, often through the internalization of the surveillance function (*Discipline and Punish*, 1975).

Chapter 5:

The Fabulous Free Market

1

Adam Smith saw the dynamics of the capitalist market economy as a product of the laws of nature. In technical language, his theory 'naturalized' the market, placing it within the purview of natural law, an ordering of nature that had been willed by God. Rationalism had not entirely eliminated the role of the divine, but it had demoted God from an active agent in the world to the position of watchmaker or architect, passively presiding over His creation – which for Smith and his followers included the capitalist market economy. If God had created capitalism, or even just the conditions under which it naturally arose, then it could only be a good thing.

It was the revolutionary notion that *good is always already taken care of within the very design of the system* that allowed Smith's successors to banish morality from economic discourse. As Spinoza might have said, nothing that happens in the market is without necessity – the economist's job is not to raise unanswerable ethical questions about market relationships, but to understand their purpose in the overall dynamic. This led to the paradoxical situation in which a so-called science of the distribution of scarce goods among competing sources of demand (a formal definition of economics) purports to be value-neutral in its work. Issues of justice in economics are shunted off to a marginal discipline known as welfare economics, or even further afield to economic philosophy. It would be as if medicine were to proceed on a value-neutral basis, inventing profitable ways to do harm with equal enthusiasm as techniques to save lives, assigning the latter to a special branch of the discipline called 'welfare medicine'.

The satirist Jonathan Swift commented memorably on the rationalist, value-neutral approach to economic thought in his famous 1729 pamphlet, 'A Modest Proposal: For Preventing the Children of Poor People in Ireland from Being a Burden to Their Parents or Country, and for Making Them Beneficial to the Publick'. After describing at some length the miserable plight of the poor and starving in Ireland, Swift presents as a perfectly rational economic strategy a plan to solve the problem, by treating children born into poverty as a readily available food source for the landed gentry:

> I have been assured by a very knowing American of my acquaintance in London, that young healthy child well nursed, is, at a year old, a most delicious nourishing and wholesome food, whether stewed, roasted, baked, or boiled; and I make no doubt that it will equally serve in a fricassee, or a ragout.

In his vicious lampoon of value-neutral economic science Swift uses statistical analysis to build an iron-clad demonstration of the utter futility of more conventional, less 'rational' social welfare approaches to the simultaneous alleviation of poverty and hunger.[1]

Swift concludes his pamphlet with a withering nod to the values of scientific objectivity:

> I profess, in the sincerity of my heart, that I have not the least personal interest in endeavoring to promote this necessary work, having no other motive than the public good of my country, by advancing our trade, providing for infants, relieving the poor, and giving some pleasure to the rich. I have no children by which I can propose to get a single penny; the youngest being nine years old, and my wife past child-bearing.[2]

The contrast between the cool reasonableness of the satire and its outrageous moral implications places in painfully sharp focus the shortcomings of an economic science that strives to synthesize moral outcomes, and which reduces people to commodities in the process. Yet even in Adam Smith's canonic *The Wealth of Nations* the necessary equilibrium of supply and demand organized by the 'invisible hand' regulates human life and death in a way that is uncomfortably akin to Swift's scandalous lampoon. Smith says:

> The demand for men, *like any other commodity*, necessarily regulates the production of men. Every species of animals naturally multiplies in proportion to their means of subsistence – [thus] among the inferior ranks of people the scantiness of subsistence sets limits to their reproduction – [which] it can do with no other way than by destroying a great part of their children.[3]

To the liberal capitalist market, even children have no value if they become a surplus commodity. Joseph Townsend (1739–1816), a cleric and dabbler in economic theory, railed against government welfare measures for the poor: 'The poor know little of the motives which stimulate the higher ranks to action – pride, honour, and ambition'. Therefore, he continued:

> The wisest legislator will never be able to devise a more equitable, a more effectual, nor in any respect a more suitable punishment, than hunger is for the disobedient servant. Hunger will tame the fiercest animals, it will teach decency and civility, obedience and subjection to the most brutish, the most obstinate, and the most perverse [...]. When hunger is either felt or feared, the desire of obtaining bread will quietly dispose the mind to undergo the greatest hardships, and will sweeten the severest labours.[4]

Similarly, David Ricardo, a leading next-generation (neo-classical) liberal economist wrote of 'the iron law of wages' (1820): 'The natural price of labour is that price which is necessary to enable the labourers, one with another, to subsist and perpetuate their race, without either increase or diminution'. Though there might be periodic economic fluctuations, brief periods of plenty, the implacable dynamics of supply and demand – i.e. natural law – would remorselessly push workers back down to penury. Despite this endemic misery, Ricardo blithely concluded that:

> [t]hese then are the laws by which wages are regulated, and by which the happiness of far the greatest part of every community is governed. Like all other contracts, wages should be left to the fair and free competition

of the market, and should never be controlled by the interference of the legislature.[5]

2

But the greatest of the neo-classical economic theorizers was William Stanley Jevons, whose *General Mathematical Theory of Political Economy* (1862) put economics on mathematical footings in a comprehensive way. Jevons saw people as 'utility-maximizing' economic agents: 'I regard man in reality as essentially selfish, that is as doing everything with a view to gain enjoyment or avoid pain [...]. This self-interest is certainly the main-spring of all his actions'.[6] Borrowing the Utilitarian idea of *pleasure* as *value*, he was able to reduce *all* sources of value in classical economics to mathematical formulae, through his ingenious theory of marginal utility.

The theory of marginal utility states that the value of any good or service is determined not by the labour or materials it embodies, but by its *utility* – by the pleasure or satisfaction it brings its purchaser. The way the market operates, he said, is that people spread their money around on various purchases in such a way that the added satisfaction gained from each of the various expenditures is equal. Where there is an imbalance among purchases, the rational individual directs more buying power towards the good or service for which desire is not yet sated, until the reward from spending just equals the cost the item purchased. Over time, everything balances out and the rational economic agent is content. That's on the demand side of the supply/demand equation: on the supply side, a business would extend its production up to the point where the cost of producing one additional unit is just the same as the income (including profit) received from that unit. In its mathematical expression, this theory is simple and elegant.

The revolutionary aspect of Jevons' formula, still central to modern economics, is that price and value are to be treated as equivalents. In other words, the value of anything in an economy is measured by its price, and vice versa. If a thing has no price, it has no value. If it does have a price, that's because it is scarce, relative to the demand for it. Air and water, being, in principle, in infinite supply and therefore not scarce, have no economic value, whereas an emerald or a ruby, which has little or no practical value, will fetch a high price due to its scarcity, and the demand for gemstones. A non-human animal has no value until it is killed and slaughtered, or made to perform some task. As historian David Noble comments, 'the concept of marginal utility [was] a universal solvent that dissolved all other human sources of value'.[7]

The neo-classical economists may have made their discipline into a mathematics-based science, but they did not entirely uncouple it from its eighteenth-century origins in theories of divine guidance tucked away within natural law. A generation after Jevons and Ricardo, the natural law approach to economic theory was as robust as ever, in the influential works of F.A. Hayek (1899–1992), a Nobel laureate. As the twentieth century's leading proponent of neo-liberal economics, and, with Milton Friedman, a stalwart of the libertarian-leaning Chicago School, Hayek wrote ecstatically of the market's 'transcendent order', to which humanity 'owes its very existence'. Market dynamics, he said, operate on a plane 'which far surpasses the reach of our understanding, wishes, and purposes' and therefore human will ought properly to be subordinated to market forces. 'Thy will (i.e. not *mine*) be done on earth as it is in heaven', he wrote of the market's supernatural authority.[8] The phrase, of course, is borrowed from the Lord's Prayer of Christian tradition, and is a profession of absolute, willing subjugation of human will to a higher power. The extract might well have been extended to include 'Give us this day our daily bread [...]' and perhaps the rest of the prayer as well.

Hayek's crypto-religious view of capitalism is especially attractive to participants in the market economy who prefer to be relieved of the burdens of conscience: in neo-liberal economics the market takes care of moral issues automatically, according to the dictates of natural law. Heretical or non-conforming viewpoints on the ordering of the world (e.g. socialism) are treated in neo-liberalism with the utmost seriousness as a threat to the true faith, and therefore to the salvation of humanity. Nations guilty of apostasy are dealt with through sanctions ranging from boycott to invasion (cf. China, Cuba, Venezuela, Chile, etc.). Since the founding of the World Bank and the International Monetary Fund in 1944, conformity has been organized and regularized through these organizations. The IMF, for example, enforces neo-liberal orthodoxy by requiring nations that borrow from it to accept more than one hundred 'conditionalities' which ensure compliance with free market conventions and practices. The ordeal of interrogation and renunciation attached to this process is not unlike that employed by the Inquisition in thirteenth-century France.[9]

Neo-liberal ideology has been characterized as a fundamentalist religion that operates in ignorance (or denial) of its own theological nature.[10] Philosopher John McMurtry notes, especially, the close fit between Hayek's free market ideology and standard definitions of theocracy, government in which clerics rule in the name of God. Each system, he reports, imposes 'a form of governance in which an infallible authority transcending human agency is represented as the ultimate regulator of daily life, with all understanding, administration and enforcement of society's rules and laws tolerated solely by compliance with the higher ruler's prescriptions'.[11] The market (and note that it is never *a* market or *our* market or *their* market; always *the* market) is tampered with by government at risk of punitive blowback, akin to what might be expected from interfering with a delicately balanced natural ecosystem.

3

Morality, in much of current economic thought, has thus been swallowed up in patterns of instrumental reason that are perfectly consistent with the seventeenth-century theories of Baruch Spinoza, for whom good is simply 'that which is certainly useful to us'. Within instrumental reason, priority in economic thought is shifted from ends to means, from the meaning and purpose behind goals to the most efficient way to attain them. In this context, so far as the market is concerned, there really is no need for moral enquiry because the market automatically produces good (i.e. moral) outcomes. No need, then, for moral reflection, or even curiosity, when we buy a pair of shoes made in some South Asian sweat-shop, or a gallon of gasoline produced from Alberta tar sands, or, for that matter, a chicken breast carved from the carcass of an animal grown in inhumane industrial conditions.

In modern economic theory, with its Utilitarian underpinnings, people are assumed to be 'rational economic agents', forever seeking to maximize their own personal gain, because doing so amounts to the satisfaction of desires, which, by definition, produces happiness. Good therefore resides in the fulfilment of desire –*any* desire – because, by definition, desired = desir*able*, or good. In other words, according to the algorithm, good is directly related to desire-satisfying consumption, which means that maximizing consumption of a desired thing maximizes good. The American economist and philosopher, Clarence Ayres, summed up the moral outlook implicit in neo-liberalism in his classic, *The Theory of Economic Progress*:

> To the question, 'What is happiness? Who shall say?' the classical econ-
> omists seemed to have found a final answer. No one can say; but no one
> *need* say, since the price system provides an instrument through the subtle
> operation of which everyone can have a say. Since consumption seems by
> axiom to be the consummation of all economic effort, and since consump-
> tion is actualized in demand, and since demand impacts upon the scarcity
> of nature to determine the form and direction of every economic under-
> taking, it seems to follow that *commerce itself expresses in this subtle fashion
> the aspirations of the race.*[12]

The fact that much of this chapter describes theoretical notions that provoke a double-take, or require a second reading on first encounter, suggests that the ideas outlined are not intuitively reasonable. Does any of it make sense? Or is liberal-capitalist economic theory an essentially perverse and inaccu-rate model of human behaviour?

NOTES

1. Jonathan Swift, "A Modest Proposal," in *The Broadview Anthology of English Literature: The Restoration and the Eighteenth Century*, ed. Joseph Black et al. (Peter-
   borough, Canada: Broadview Press, 2009), 418. An excerpt provides the flavour:

   > The number of souls in this kingdom being usually reckoned one million
   > and a half, of these I calculate there may be about two hundred thousand
   > couples whose wives are breeders; from which number I subtract thirty
   > thousand couples who are able to maintain their own children, although
   > I apprehend there cannot be so many, under the present distresses of the
   > kingdom; but this being granted, there will remain a hundred and seventy
   > thousand breeders. I again subtract fifty thousand for those women who
   > miscarry, or whose children die by accident or disease within the year.
   > There only remains one hundred and twenty thousand children of poor
   > parents annually born. The question therefore is, how this number shall
   > be reared and provided for, which, as I have already said, under the pres-
   > ent situation of affairs, is utterly impossible by all the methods hitherto
   > proposed [...] of the hundred and twenty thousand children already
   > computed, twenty thousand may be reserved for breed[ing], whereof only

one-fourth part to be males; which is more than we allow to sheep, black cattle or swine; and my reason is, that these children are seldom the fruits of marriage, a circumstance not much regarded by our savages; therefore, one male will be sufficient to serve four females. That the remaining hundred thousand may, at a year old, be offered in the sale to the persons of quality and fortune through the kingdom; always advising the mother to let them suck plentifully in the last month, so as to render them plump and fat for a good table. A child will make two dishes at an entertainment for friends; and when the family dines alone, the fore or hind quarter will make a reasonable dish, and seasoned with a little pepper or salt will be very good boiled on the fourth day, especially in winter.

2. Swift, "A Modest Proposal," 419. See also George Wittkowsky, "Swift's Modest Proposal: The Biography of an Early Georgian Pamphlet," *Journal of the History of Ideas* 4, no. 1 (1943): 75–104.

3. Swift, "A Modest Proposal," 419. See also Wittkowsky, "Swift's Modest Proposal" and Smith, *Wealth of Nations*, 50. Emphasis added.

4. Joseph Townsend, "A Dissertation on the Poor Laws, By a Well-Wisher to Mankind" (Gale Ecco, 1786).

5. David Ricardo, *The Works of David Ricardo* (London: John Murray, 1871), 57.

6. W. S. Jevons, *Papers and Correspondence of William Stanley Jevons, Volumes I–VII*, ed. R. D. Collison Black and Rosamund Könekamp (London: Macmillan Press, 1972), Vol. I: 133.

7. David F. Noble, *Beyond the Promised Land: The Movement and the Myth* (Toronto: Harlequin Enterprises, 2006).

8. Friedrich Hayek, *The Fatal Conceit* (New York: Routledge, 1988), 6–7, 74, 130–31. Emphasis and brackets in the original. See also his more famous *Road to Serfdom* (London: Routledge, 1943).

9. Greg Palast, "The Globalizer Who Came in from the Cold," *The Observer*, October 10, 2001.

10. John McMurtry, "Understanding Market Theology," in *The Invisible Hand and the Common Good*, ed. Bernard Hodgson (New York: Springer, 2004), 152.

11. McMurtry, "Understanding Market Theology," 181.

12. Clarence Ayres, *The Theory of Economic Progress* (Chapel Hill: University of North Carolina Press, 1944), ch. 4.

Chapter 6:

On a Treadmill to Happiness

1

Reducing the idea of good to the satisfaction of desires – any and all desires – is central to modern economic theory. It is also as radical a form of moral relativism as one could imagine. Defining good in terms of the satisfaction of individuals' desires for market commodities, of course, sidesteps any consideration of deeper values and interests, such as whether the true constituents of one's self-interest are to be found within the market's material domain, or if it might be possible, even commonplace, for individuals to desire what is not in their best interest to have. Is what one desires always what one ought to desire, or might there be a worthwhile distinction to be made? What about the interests of others as they may be affected by my consumption?

While there clearly is a connection between well-being (or happiness) and getting what you want, the linkage, as famously rendered in St. Augustine, is more complex than what is imagined by economists. Freely translated, Augustine says:

> All those are truly fortunate who have what they desire, although not all who have what they desire are therefore fortunate. But they are clearly wretched, who either do not have what they desire, or have that which they do not rightly desire. Therefore, he only is a fortunate (blessed) man, who both has all things which he desires, and desires nothing ill.[1]

It sounds like a riddle, but it makes perfect sense. Good fortune, or happiness, is dependent not just on getting what you want; it depends on both getting what you want and wanting the right things. Wanting the wrong things and getting them is not a recipe for happiness.

What are the right things to want? What is meant by morally justifiable desires? Market theory cannot help us with those questions; nevertheless, their significance cannot be denied. First of all, in Augustine's formulation, which is so intuitively clear it might be called an axiom, happiness is in some measure dependent on correct moral decision-making. Second, philosophers and psychologists agree that it is through the very process of making considered choices among one's wants and desires – discovering and prioritizing what is of value – that we create an identity, a self.[2] This is how we discover what is truly important to us, truly significant in our lives.

In making these choices we construct our core identity. It goes without saying that those choices will not be made exclusively, or even usually, on the economic basis of cost versus expected utility, on the basis of value for money. That is, they will not be made on a purely instrumental, economic basis, but rather according to a set of criteria that includes moral values and is rooted ultimately in a notion of good that transcends economics.

Much more could be said of the wobbly philosophical and 'scientific' stilts on which liberal capitalist economic theory has been teetering. In the end, it is abundantly clear that these theories, particularly as they found expression in liberal, laissez-faire ideology, were more than anything else an elegant justification for the political and economic interests of the newly powerful merchant and business classes in the eighteenth- and early-nineteenth-century Europe. The historian Jacques Droz has encapsulated it well:

> The bourgeoisie, while industrial development was enabling it to increase its income slowly but surely, declared itself to be satisfied with the normal operation of supply and demand. Unaffected by the growing misery of the masses, it contented itself with preaching charity, thrift and celibacy; besides, it believed that technical advances would make possible a progressive improvement in general well-being. As for forms of government, the best was that which disturbed the bourgeois least in his accumulation of wealth.[3]

Successive generations of economists believed, with Adam Smith, that the troubling conflicts presented by the liberal market (e.g. income disparity) arose as the result of inescapable economic principles and were therefore unavoidable. As subscribers to natural law theory they believed, with Spinoza, that '[n]othing happens in nature which might be attributed to any defect in it'.[4] Thomas Malthus (1766–1834) wrote: 'The people must regard themselves as being themselves the principal cause of their misfortunes'. Another leading economist of the day, John McCulloch (1789–1864), seconded him, and argued that inescapable natural law guaranteed the failure of social welfare measures on behalf of the poor and disadvantaged; the best that could be hoped of well-intentioned welfare laws was that they would be ineffectual and therefore not disruptive of market dynamics. Economists and politicians of a similar mindset are not hard to find today.

There is no escaping the fact that liberal economic theory, despite its long-standing ambition to become the hard-core physics of the social sciences, the authoritative discipline to which all others must bow, is flawed and deeply deficient in its prescriptions for achieving human happiness. It could scarcely be otherwise, given its refusal to consider moral realities and their implications in its teaching and practice. The truth is that no matter how it twists and turns, no matter how well it cloaks itself in mathematical formulae and axioms, contemporary economic theory cannot escape the moral questions for which it has no coherent answers.

2

Psychologists agree that a view of the world that is solidly grounded in the real and the true is the cognitive foundation on which happiness is built – if only because it curbs unrealizable expectations. So, to the degree that market ideology misrepresents the meaning of happiness and its sources, it is likely to be a cause of *un*happiness. Nevertheless, most of us subscribe to it in our day-to-day lives, because success and prosperity, even social acceptance, demand that we do so. If we are to survive and thrive we have no choice but to accept major tenets of the capitalist market ideology at least some of the time, tolerating and even foregrounding our selfish, acquisitive, envious, competitive and aggressive impulses. We are forced somehow to cope with the painful disconnect between that theory-laden world-view and the one we know in our bones to be more in keeping with everyday human experience.

In his exhaustive survey of sociological findings on happiness in market democracies, Yale political scientist Robert E. Lane concludes:

> Amidst the satisfaction people feel with their material progress, there is a spirit of unhappiness and depression haunting advanced market democracies throughout the world, a spirit that mocks the idea that markets maximize well-being and the 18th century promise of a right to the pursuit of happiness under benign governments of people's own choosing.

The discontent has diverse symptoms. They include, as Lane reports:

> [a] postwar decline in the United States in people who report themselves as happy, a rising tide in all advanced societies of clinical depression and dysphoria (especially among the young), increasing distrust of each other and of political and other institutions, declining belief that the lot of the average man is getting better, a tragic erosion of family solidarity and community integration together with an apparent decline in warm, intimate relations among friends.[5]

Multiple surveys beginning with the early post-Second World War years and continuing to the present show that, beyond the level at which basic necessities are met, rising incomes and the things they allow people to buy have little or no correlation with subjective feelings of well-being, or happiness. Other, similarly comprehensive studies show that community and companionship, friendship and community esteem and strong familial bonds are all strongly related to happiness. The evidence is convincing enough for Lane to conclude that 'the way to increase [subjective well-being] in the United States and probably in all advanced Western societies is to move from an emphasis on money and economic growth toward an emphasis on companionship'.[6]

It is not markets, but things external to the market that provide happiness. Money, or material gain, appears to have a declining marginal utility, meaning that as people acquire more of this specific good it loses value for them compared to other, scarcer goods, which in turn increase in value. In other words, the more material wealth one accumulates, the less value it has, a phenomenon Lane has dubbed 'the hedonic treadmill'. With some possible qualifications, the same does not appear to be true of friendship, community and family.

Many people would challenge this conclusion, arguing that money can indeed buy happiness. But surveys aimed specifically at probing the truth of this time-worn trope have found that even strong believers in the money–happiness relationship do not *themselves* find sustained happiness in increased wealth (though there may be brief periods when money does give intense happiness). Researchers conclude that the powerful, ubiquitous, ideological reinforcement that is characteristic of market societies and their media helps to explain the paradox that *despite the evidence of their own experience*, many people continue to pursue the pipe dream of happiness through wealth. It's a condition that Lane labels the 'economistic fallacy'.[7]

There is another, even more interesting, reason why people persist in their belief that happiness flows from wealth: Lane reports that 'official economic doctrine denies them the belief that many of their main pleasures in life come from their work'. Economists going all the way back to Jeremy Bentham, the Utilitarian philosopher, have treated work as a disutility – the pain that must be endured to get to the pleasures of consumption. Bentham wrote:

> Desire for labour *for the sake of labour* – of labour considered in the char-acter of an *end*, without any view to anything else – is a sort of desire that seems scarcely to have a place in the human breast [...]. *Aversion* – not *desire* – is the only emotion which labour, taken by itself, is qualified to produce [...] ease not labour, is the object. Love of labour is a contradiction in terms.[8]

The idea that work must be a disutility is so patently false that it is difficult to understand how Bentham and succeeding generations of economists (many of whom laboured happily over their tracts and papers) could have seriously entertained it. Yet, it has remained intrinsic to economic theory. This, in the face of reliable current evidence that people rank a sense of constructive accomplishment (a sense of efficacy) six times higher than money in terms of well-being.[9]

It is not unreasonable to blame this perspective on labour for the otherwise incomprehensible current practice of rewarding senior corporate managers (and now government bureaucrats, too) with staggering bonuses simply for doing their jobs. The notion that many of them might find their positions intrinsically rewarding and satisfying simply does not compute in modern text-book wisdom. Nor does the idea that, if it is necessary to pay a senior manager enormous bonuses to remain on the job, perhaps he or she is the wrong person for that job! At a minimum, the Utilitarian theory of the essential disutility of work, however mistaken, provides a theoretically defensible fig leaf for what otherwise seems an unjustifiable misappropriation of corporate wealth and government funds.

It is worth noting, in passing, that the evidence Lane has compiled indicates that although intimacy through community, friends and family is crucial to mental health and the avoidance of depression, it is not the case that friendship 'networks' – one thinks of Facebook or Snapchat – can provide a substitute. Even among the young, popularity is no replacement for closeness:

> [S]tudents want confidants, people in whom they can confide, more than friends with whom they can 'hang out'. Is that because they are young? Not at all: the importance of intimacy actually increases from youth to middle life […]. It might be that market relations increase networks (they are so useful), but it is doubtful that they encourage intimacy (partly because it is so time-consuming).[10]

Lane's own survey-based research indicates a clear trend away from intimacy in market societies, and towards what he calls Machiavellian relationships with others. Pressures generated by the market, along with urbanization and industrialization, lead people increasingly to value relationships in terms of their instrumental usefulness, so that they tend to have more and more acquaintances and fewer and fewer close confidants. The same pressures weaken family relationships as well: 'Throughout the world, the main cost of the imposition of modern market and technological patterns on traditional patterns has been the disruption of interpersonal, especially family, relations', Lane reports.[11] He sees in the mountains of statistical evidence he has amassed a vicious cycle at work:

> (1) [M]aterialism does not lead to life satisfaction or happiness; (2) unhappiness, and especially depression, leads to withdrawal and tends to alienate people; (3) lack of companionship – and companionship is a genuine, if

subordinated value for materialists – contributes further to the materialist's unhappiness [...]. Materialists, economic men, endowed with the qualities that economists assume are the characteristics of winners, tend, in fact, to be losers from the start.[12]

Market economies may have made us prosperous, but they do not maximize utility or the satisfaction of human wants in anything but an instrumentalist, Utilitarian sense. In other words, not in real life.

Continuing changes in the fundamental dynamics of market capitalism, brought about by the rise of the modern business corporation, have only served to further distort this relationship. That is the subject of the next chapter.

NOTES

1. St. Augustine, *The City of God* (ca. 420 CE).
2. See, for example, Charles Taylor, *Sources of the Self* (Cambridge: Harvard University Press, 1989).
3. Jacques Droz, *Europe Between Revolutions 1815–1848* (New York, Fontana Books, 1981), 45.
4. Baruch Spinoza, *Ethica* (1677).
5. Robert E. Lane, *The Loss of Happiness in Market Democracies* (New Haven: Yale University Press, 2000), 3.
6. Lane, *The Loss of Happiness in Market Democracies*, 7.
7. Lane, *The Loss of Happiness in Market Democracies*, 141ff.
8. Stark, ed., *Jeremy Bentham's Economic Writings*, 427–28. Emphasis in original.
9. Lane, *The Loss of Happiness in Market Democracies*, 73.
10. Lane, *The Loss of Happiness in Market Democracies*, 80.
11. Lane, *The Loss of Happiness in Market Democracies*, 117.
12. Lane, *The Loss of Happiness in Market Democracies*, 158.

Chapter 7:

The Corporate Takeover

1

Bit by bit, one court case at a time, market capitalism fundamentally transformed itself during the first two-thirds of the twentieth century. The metamorphosis was below the radar of all but specialist observers, but it may be the ultimate triumph of rationalist economic thinking. The transformative difference is the hegemony of the modern business corporation in domestic markets of the world's wealthiest nations, and in the international markets they share.

As wealth and market power were increasingly consolidated in the hands of fewer and fewer enormous corporations, the troubling disconnect between the canonic assumption of consistently self-interested behaviour by market participants (i.e. people), and their often idiosyncratic behaviour in practice, was dramatically narrowed. Business corporations, acting as proxies for millions of individual shareholders, reliably behaved the way rational economic agents were supposed to. Today, these financial and industrial behemoths enjoy surprising privileges and exert enormous influence over every aspect of our lives. And yet as the daily news attests, they, and their senior managers, routinely behave with shocking, seemingly sociopathic irresponsibility.[1] How are we to account for this?

The term 'modern business corporation' has a specific meaning that needs to be defined. First of all, it does not include the small to medium-sized corporations owned and operated by their founders or their successors as family concerns or partnerships. Numerically, these are by far the majority in the world of corporate business. What the term is intended to signify is the large business corporation that is no longer privately held, but listed on stock exchanges and owned by a large number of shareholders, a group that typically includes other corporate institutions such as pension funds, mutual funds, insurance companies and the like.

Management positions in the modern business corporation are occupied almost exclusively by university-trained professionals whose fiduciary mandate is to serve the interests of the shareholders. Serving the shareholders is taken to mean one thing: maximizing the return on their investment. This in turn means maximizing corporate profit.

I have called these entities *cyber-corporations* to draw attention to their novelty, and because at their core they are essentially machine entities that regulate their own operations through feedback from their environment. They are, in other words, cybernetic mechanisms, and within them human 'management' is confined to narrowly prescribed roles that are delineated by the algorithms governing the corporate machine's legal and financial existence.

The large business corporation of today had its genesis as a straightforward legal resource for the accumulation of capital. As the booming capitalist economy of Europe spun its colonizing web across continents and oceans to Africa, Asia and the New World in the sixteenth and seventeenth centuries, the potential for realizing vast wealth through trade and commerce was undercut by the enormous risks involved in such far-flung ventures. A solution was found by lawyers, entrepreneurs and politicians in the joint-stock corporation, in which individual investors were sheltered from the full impact of financial disaster brought on by, for example, the loss of a ship, or the extermination of a colony or trading outpost by disease or hostile indigenous peoples. A tool developed mainly in Britain, these entities operated under royal charters, and often served vital foreign policy interests such as colonization.[2]

In these new 'limited-liability' corporations, investors' exposure to liability for unpaid loans, lawsuits, and other claims against the corporation was restricted, by law, to the amount of their personal investment. That is, no single investor could be called to account for financial loss or indebtedness incurred by the corporate entity, beyond what he or she had invested. An individual investor thus could look to the potential of enormous returns, at relatively low risk. This amounted to a way of socializing risk while privatizing profit, because it frequently fell to outside interests, usually state governments, to deal with the fallout of financial disaster. But it spurred the rapid development of capitalism and its markets by making possible the accumulation of large pools of private capital which were managed by trained professionals.

During the late nineteenth century, business corporations sought and were granted new privileges, beyond limited liability. In a succession of court cases in the United States and Britain they were freed from restrictive charters that had limited them to the single, specific enterprise for which they were incorporated, freeing them to deploy their capital as they pleased. They successfully petitioned the courts for formal legal recognition of their ancient, unofficial identity as 'persons' in matters of law and regulation. Then, leveraging their statutory personhood, they began an ultimately successful campaign in American courts to attain essentially the same human rights protections and remedies as are enjoyed by human beings under the Bill of Rights.

As the twentieth century drew to a close, corporations had gained access to the protections of the First, Fourth, Fifth, Sixth and Seventh Amendments, which cover the right to free speech; freedom from unreasonable searches and searches without warrants; freedom from double jeopardy; and the right to trial by jury in both criminal and civil cases. These rights were extended internationally using the leverage of international trade agreements and institutions.

The capstone of the transformation came in 2010 with the US Supreme Court's ruling in the Citizens United case, which overturned federal legislation restricting corporate spending during elections. The court found that limiting corporations' spending of money to support a cause amounted to restraining free speech, which is protected under the First Amendment. The result has been to exacerbate an already serious problem of corporate money determining election outcomes, and it requires a formal constitutional amendment to overrule the court.

The divorce of ownership from management functions, the single-minded goal of maximizing profit, the freedom to engage in any field of business, and the ability to challenge government authority from behind the shield of human rights statutes have combined to make the modern business corporation something unique in history. Designed initially as a tool for making money, it has evolved into a highly complex legal entity that is essentially robotic in character. Its goal remains the same – maximizing return on shareholder investment – but its power and influence have been enormously enlarged, and not just its influence on the outside world, but on its workers and managers as well.

2

Over the past half-century, sophisticated management techniques and new surveillance technologies have combined to impose internal controls regulating corporate employee behaviour at every level, from the shop floor to the corner C-suites. So effective are these tools that today it seems impossible to avoid the conclusion that the corporate entity per se manages its managers, confining them to modes of behaviour that are defined entirely by the instrumental needs and goals of the corporation. Those who do not fit this mold are either re-educated to conformity through various forms of coercion and persuasion, or weeded out.

The situation of humans within the corporate entity is in many ways analogous to the role of modern military personnel, who often operate within an environment defined by the needs and objectives of their weapons systems: 'The [human] aircrew of the Apache [attack helicopter] is expected to function reliably as an extension of such machines [...] or weapons systems generally; [as] adjunct for some limitation the machine has due to its incomplete development'.[3] The 'machine', in the case of the modern business corporation, is the organizational structure, or bureaucracy, that defines its existence. It is the very close integration of machine and human elements of the system which suggests the term cyber-corporation to distinguish these modern innovations from their evolutionary predecessors. As with the military machine, a goal of the cyber-corporation is to replace humans with robots to the extent feasible.

University researchers have for some time been seriously examining modern business corporations as examples of a wider, cross-disciplinary research category called 'self-organizing systems'. The studies draw on biologists' study of 'collective beings', which are defined as complex, goal-oriented, self-organizing systems made up of large numbers of autonomous entities.[4] In the study of collective beings, theories of self-organization and computer modelling are employed in an attempt to understand how large numbers of autonomous creatures – bees in hives, or ants in their colonies, or birds in flocks, or fish in schools – can exhibit highly coordinated behaviour without apparent overall management. A promising line of enquiry is found in *emergence theory*, a field of physics (and a branch of chaos theory) that studies the 'emergent properties' of highly complex systems, as, for example, the spontaneous emergence of tornados from certain weather patterns, or the spontaneous emergence of consciousness from billions of neurons in our brains, or the similarly spontaneous emergence of life from complex chemical soups. A feature of emergent properties is that they often have the ability to influence and even control the very systems that spawned them.

Applied to the cyber-corporation, the new disciplines suggest that these huge bureaucracies are more than the sum of their parts: they need to be understood as systems made up of autonomous individuals (i.e. workers and managers) whose behaviour on the job is governed both by initial design parameters, and an emergent property that could be called a culture. Within the system, human managers are made to conform to the cyber-corporation's goals and values, rather than vice versa.

The antisocial behaviour of so many of the world's largest corporations in every field from communications and media to pharmaceuticals to agribusiness and forestry, to mining, to automobile manufacturing, to finance etc. is less baffling if seen in the context of the mature cyber-corporation as a machine-like, self-regulating organism. It is designed to maximize the value of the assets under its control, on behalf of its shareholders; external considerations, up to and including human life, are factored into its decision-making only to the extent that they may have an impact on that goal, positive or negative.[5] Interventions by human actors within the machine are limited both by the fear of getting fired, and a kind of cultivated moral myopia. According to David Luban, there are at least three ways in which corporate structures mute any sense of moral culpability:

> Psychologically, role players in such organizations lack the emotional sense that they are morally responsible for the consequences of organizational behaviour [...]. Politically, responsibility cannot be located on the organizational chart and thus in some real way no one – *no one* – ever is responsible. Morally, role players have insufficient information to be confident that they are in a position to deliberate effectively

because bureaucratic organizations parcel out information along functional lines.[6]

3

In the corporate-capitalist economy as it is configured today worldwide, it is more difficult than ever to see how moral outcomes might emerge, spontaneously and autonomously, from the dynamics of the system. The cyber-corporation has usurped the classical economist's idealized market of many small companies competing on more or less equal terms with one another for customers and raw materials, serving well-informed consumers who are making 'rational' decisions. If that highly idealized market ever existed as the norm, it no longer does. The cyber-corporation has expanded the once tightly regulated corporate niche in the market to occupy the entire organism, like a virulent parasite.

Not only does the cyber-corporation determine what goods and services the market supplies (i.e. those that are most profitable), it shapes demand through the mass media it owns or controls. The market can no longer reasonably be said to operate in the interests of citizens (now called 'consumers' and 'human resources'). It has long since turned to serving the interests of the cyber-corporations that inhabit it. To the degree that the market orchestrates the satisfaction of desires, it is the desires of the cyber-corporation that are chiefly served, and these resolve themselves into a single consideration: profit.

Looked at another way, the cyber-corporation represents the realization of classical economists' idealized understanding of people as primarily self-interested, pleasure-seeking individuals. Within the modern, liberal capitalist system, the interests of shareholders (whether personal or institutional) are represented collectively in the market by the cyber-corporation, which actually does fit the model of incorrigible self-interest and endless acquisitiveness. It is the ultimate 'rational economic agent'.

If there was ever a time when humanity could look to the market as a reasonable proxy for the moral systems of earlier eras, that time is over. As the next chapter will show, with the cyber-corporation in the driver's seat, market economies in their ever-increasing speed and efficiency are operating in a world of moral weightlessness, where in the absence of gravity, 'Things fall apart; the centre cannot hold'.[7]

NOTES

1. See Wade Rowland, *Greed, Inc.: Why Corporations Rule Our World* (Toronto: Thomas Allen Publishers, 2005; New York: Arcade Publishers, 2006, 2012).

2. Examples are the Hudson Bay Company, the East India Company, the Massachusetts Bay Company and the Virginia Company.

3. Lawrence Radine, *The Taming of the Troops: Social Control in the U.S. Army* (New York: Greenwood, 1977), 89.

4. See Rowland, *Greed, Inc.* For an extensive introduction to the sciences of emergence, see Mark A. Bedau and Paul Humphreys, *Emergence: Contemporary Readings in Philosophy and Science* (Cambridge: MIT Press, 2008). For more on the emergence, see Melanie Mitchell, *Complexity: A Guided Tour* (New York: Oxford University Press, 2009).

5. Cyber-corporations, in their early appearances as actors in emerging, rapidly expanding markets (e.g. Bell Telephone at the beginning of the twentieth century, or Google at the century's end), may sometimes seem to have diverse social interests beyond profit. However as the organization matures along with its market, those experimental interests, which are typically unorthodox, untested approaches to profitability, tend to vanish, along with their champions, in the process of continuous rationalization.

6. David Luban, *Lawyers and Justice* (Princeton: Princeton University Press, 1989), 123.

7. W. B. Yeats, "The Second Coming," (1920).

Chapter 8:

The Tragedy of the Commons

1

Thomas Carlyle, the Scottish historian and chronicler of the French Revolution, famously referred to the discipline of economics as it was emerging in his time as 'the dismal science'. Though the context in which he used the phrase now seems bizarre (he was arguing for the reintroduction of slavery in the West Indies), it caught on and has since been borrowed by a thousand other writers to describe what they see as economic science rooted in implacable rules of necessity.

In the 1960s and 1970s the phrase was picked up by editorialists and applied to the blossoming field of environmental science instead for raising questions about the sustainability of current economic practices. Paul Ehrlich's *The Population Bomb*, the Club of Rome's *Limits to Growth* and other books in the same vein did indeed make gloomy reading, as did a highly influential essay by biologist and ecologist Garrett Hardin, entitled 'The Tragedy of the Commons'. With historian Lynn White's essay 'The Historic Roots of Our Ecologic Crisis' and Aldo Leopold's much older book, *A Sand County Almanac*, Hardin's essay, first published in the journal *Science*, is often identified as one of a handful of seminal documents that launched the field of environmental ethics.

Hardin's tract was firmly in the eighteenth-century rationalist tradition. As a disciple of the more deterministic fringes of sociobiology, his concerns about overpopulation led him to hold controversial opinions on abortion and immigration. On the former, he observed:

[A] medical abortion, particularly in the early stages, costs only a fraction as much as a medically supported childbirth – not to mention the costs of education and other social services to the child for 18 years. So: when a woman elects to have a child, she is committing the community to something like $100,000 in expenses for the bearing and rearing of that child. Is it wise to extend individual rights that far?[1]

He was well known for his advocacy of 'lifeboat ethics', which, like triage in a hospital emergency ward, calculates costs and benefits before determining who should receive life-giving support. On this basis, he favoured tightly restricting immigration to the United States. He argued that reducing infant mortality worldwide would be disastrous for the human species. He and his wife were both members of the Hemlock Society, which advocated legalizing assisted suicide. The two took their own lives in their California home in 2003 shortly after celebrating their sixty-second wedding anniversary: she was 82; he was 88.

These details of Hardin's life illustrate an ideological perspective nowadays referred to as *scientistic*, denoting an extreme materialism or positivism expressed in an excessive faith in the power and utility of scientific knowledge and beliefs. It is helpful to have this background in looking into his most influential essay.

The 'Tragedy of the Commons' proposes a scenario that, on first reading, seems diametrically opposed to the classical economist's idea of the invisible hand of the market turning individual self-interest into communal welfare. For this reason, it caused considerable excitement among the 1970s counter-culture environmentalists. Here was a seemingly irrefutable argument against prevailing capitalist market theory, proof that the consumer society was unsustainable. It also suggested that laissez-faire market capitalism did not provide a sure-fire path to the greatest happiness for the greatest number, as conventional theory claimed.

The essay begins with an epigraph in which Hardin quotes himself: 'The population problem has no technical solution; it requires a fundamental extension in morality'. By the end of the essay, the reader understands that what he means by 'extension of morality' is a Utilitarian-style replacement of authentic morality with instrumental logic.

Hardin starts by arguing that human populations will never settle at some optimum, sustainable point as was predicted in classical and neoclassical economics. 'We can make little progress in working toward optimum population size until we explicitly exorcize the spirit of Adam Smith [...]', he stated. That spirit has 'contributed to a dominant tendency of thought that has ever since interfered with positive action based on rational analysis [...]'. If Smith's assumption that private self-interest leads to public welfare via the invisible hand is correct, Hardin wrote, 'it justifies the continuance of our present policy of laissez-faire in reproduction [...] if the assumption is not correct, we need to reexamine our individual freedoms to see which ones are defensible'.[2]

Hardin wanted that re-examination for reasons he presented in the form of a parable about a common pasture and a group of herdsmen who share it to graze their cattle:

> Such an arrangement may work reasonably satisfactorily for centuries because tribal wars, poaching, and disease keep the numbers of both man and beast well below the carrying capacity of the land. Finally, however, comes the day of reckoning, that is, the day when the long-desired goal of social stability becomes a reality.

It is at this point, Hardin said, that 'the inherent logic of the commons remorselessly generates tragedy'.

What happens is this: each herdsman will rationally examine his position *vis a vis* the common pasture and see that if he adds one more steer to his herd, all of the cattle grazing there will have slightly less to eat, and the land itself will be under a little more stress, but the loss will be more than compensated for him, as an individual, because he reaps the full benefit of the sale of the extra steer. In other words, the positive impact on his position will be something close to +1, while the negative impact will be only a small fraction of –1. Hardin explains:

> But this is the conclusion reached by each and every rational herdsman sharing a commons. Therein is the tragedy. Each man is locked into a system that compels him to increase his herd without limit – in a world that is limited. Ruin is the destination towards which all men rush, each pursuing his own best interest in a society that believes in the freedom of the commons. Freedom in a commons will bring ruin to all.[3]

Hardin goes on to say that just such a tragedy is currently brewing worldwide due to the fact that we treat the air and water as a commons, with the result that polluters continue to dump their wastes there, to the point of environmental disaster in the form of global warming, desertification of the seas and other disasters. He also claims that his parable demonstrates that, without regulation, and according to the same herdsman's logic, people will continue to breed without restraint until the world's maximum sustainable population is exceeded, and population collapse ensues.

2

Hardin's parable has been justly criticized over the years for presenting human behaviour much as Hobbes had, entirely constrained by innate and unavoidable 'natural' responses to the environment. (He is simply wrong, for example, about the dynamics of population growth.) Note the language he uses: we are 'locked into' a system that 'compels' certain behaviour. Most of us would agree, to the contrary, that humans are capable of behaving sensibly and charitably when faced with a situation such as Hardin sketches, and of acting in the interest of the wider community. In fact this would seem to be, by any objective measurement, our normal mode of behaviour. We humans are prone to altruism, or concern for the other.

Nor does historical evidence support his defeatist outlook. As Jared Diamond notes in his book *Collapse*, for example, Icelandic shepherds of six centuries ago saw that overgrazing was threatening the country's sparse highland pasture land with irreversible erosion. They responded, not as Hardin would have predicted, but by joining together to determine how many sheep the land could support, and assigning quotas among themselves. The fourth-millennium BC Sumerians, on the other hand, did indeed destroy their civilization – the world's first – by overexploiting their arable land. But in their case the danger was not something readily understandable to them. The slow process of salinization of the land caused by too much irrigation was a complex hydrological process that would not be unravelled until the advent of modern science-based agriculture. Where the risk to communal assets is evident and understood, people have historically demonstrated a capacity to suppress short-term avarice and to cooperate in the achievement of a longer-term common good.

There is, however, one important actor in our market economy that *does* match Hardin's depiction of the incorrigibly rational, self-interested economic agent, and that is the cyber-corporation we met in the previous chapter. Wherever the cyber-corporation dominates a commons, the tragedy

Hardin depicts is highly likely to be the outcome. The fact that fish stocks are collapsing in the world's oceans due to overfishing is directly related to the fact that by far the biggest players in the world's fisheries are cyber-corporations. The 'soil mining' that results in soil exhaustion and widespread erosion throughout the world is carried on not by individual farmers, but by the mammoth corporations that dominate agribusiness. Mining of mineral deposits in ways that despoil the environment is carried out almost exclusively by the cyber-corporations that dominate the mineral extraction industry. Political measures to control global warming by curbing greenhouse gas emissions are resisted and actively undermined not by individual people, but by the globalized corporations that dominate the fossil energy industry, and pool their resources to establish phony 'public advocacy' groups. Where self-employed individuals are directly responsible for damaging the common, as, for example, in the case of farmers or ranchers using slash-and-burn techniques in rain forests, it is invariably the cyber-corporations that create the market conditions that encourage these practices.

This is not simply a matter of scale. Certainly, the cyber-corporation is typically very large and powerful. But the problem is that, whatever its size and influence, it has no concern for the human interest. As an essentially machine entity, it is not susceptible to feelings of compassion, of shame or pride, of charity or love. Where healthy humans will voluntarily curb their behaviour if they can see that it is harming their neighbour, cyber-corporations alter their behaviour solely according to impact on profit. While they typically present themselves through their public relations divisions as caring, compassionate players in the market, concerned with human welfare at various levels, they do this quite transparently in a bid to maximize profit by cultivating a congenial image.

To put it another way, the cyber-corporation is not interested in virtuous behaviour, only in the *appearance* of virtue, which is reputation. A good reputation is profitable; a bad one is not. For this reason, the cyber-corporation's 'virtuous' actions never go unannounced, unpublicized, unadvertised, even though we humans consider virtue to be its own reward, and admire most that virtue which is private and unannounced. This is why the cyber-corporation will continue to mine the world's soils and oceans, to dump harmful chemicals into waterways and the atmosphere, to promote the use of dangerous drugs in inappropriate conditions, to exploit adult and child workers, to seek profit from sickness, war, and natural disaster and to expose society to the unintended consequences of inadequately tested technologies – unless faced with strictly enforced regulations that impose penalties that are greater than the financial gains achieved through their antisocial behaviour.

There are, of course, rare exceptions in which corporate profit-making somehow aligns with morally and environmentally responsible behaviour, but these tend to be confined to niche areas of existing industries, and serve customers who are seeking ethical alternatives. However, as a rational economic agent, the typical cyber-corporation will operate at and beyond the limits of law and regulation (maximizing 'pleasure') so long as it is profitable to do so. It is not susceptible to moral suasion, except occasionally through boycotts and other forms of consumer revolt, and in this sense there is no such thing as a 'good corporate citizen'. Corporate social responsibility, a hot topic in business schools everywhere, can be a reality only if it is imposed from outside, through some mechanism that affects profit, in which case compliant behaviour on the part of the cyber-corporation is 'responsible' only in the narrow sense of being protective of its own interests. It may be socially responsible in its effect, but not in its intent.

Those who have an itch to curb the frequently sociopathic behaviour of the cyber-corporation should therefore focus their interest not only on corporate management technique, but also on public administration and politics. If the unfettered mechanisms of the market do not deliver communal welfare as promised, then no amount of corporate management expertise will alter that reality; in fact the more effective and efficient corporate managers become – the better they do their job – the more powerful and therefore potentially dangerous the corporations themselves become. Yes, large corporations do create wealth from which not just shareholders but the larger society benefits. But there are other ways to create wealth, and more effective ways to distribute it. That, however, is a different topic.

The tragedy of the commons is real, but it is not the tragedy of classical drama, of human beings living out their lives in the grip of ineluctable fate, unable to escape their destinies. It is a robo-tragedy created by amoral, machine-like institutions of our own design that have been set loose upon the world in ignorance of the eventual consequences. It is a tragedy of blind faith in reason, in technology and in the tools we engineer in order to manipulate the world around us.

3

The last word we can (unfashionably) leave to Aristotle and his perennial wisdom. For Aristotle, the science of moral living, the highest of all disciplines, is the study of politics, and vice versa. It would be foolish to suggest that his prescriptions for good governance ought to be adopted in the contemporary world, or even that they are capable of being adapted to our much more complex situation. But they do have value as a sounding board, as great, eternal ideas against which others can be measured and weighed. Other, more contemporary thinkers may have ideas of more direct application to today's situation, but we are interested here in getting back to basics, for the very good reason that we have evidently lost sight of the kinds of important fundamental realities that so concerned the ancients.

What we learn from Aristotle is that morality, while it is ultimately rooted in a universal good (as seen in Plato), is nonetheless a matter for local interpretation, and therefore it is, in its detailed application, a social enterprise. The moral individual must be well-versed in these real-life distinctions, and so it follows that no person can hope to lead a virtuous life without being embedded from childhood in a moral community. While we may emerge from the womb equipped with a basic moral grammar, the way it is articulated depends on our community: without community involvement, it may not develop at all.

For Aristotle, the individual can find ultimate fulfilment only in the community, which, for him, was the city-state. This is because being a moral person and doing good are one and the same: morality is a matter of action within a social environment. One can be stuffed with moral theory and abstract ethical ideas, but to *be* a moral person one must make real moral choices and act on them. Morality, which is subsumed by the science of politics, is a *practical* science in that its pursuit is not one of theory, but of action.

We are all moral creatures, Aristotle believed, born that way, but the only way for a young person to learn to be moral in practice – to learn moral *behaviour* – is to observe the actions of moral persons in his or her community. Political science will be able to discover true moral universals through the study of what various communities consider to be moral behaviour, but while theoretical education can be helpful, it is not essential to becoming a moral person, he believed. The key to morality in both the individual and the community is upbringing, and early familiarity with the watchwords of morality – the *seemly* (or virtuous), and the *just*: 'It makes no small difference, then whether we form [moral] habits of one kind or another from our very youth; it makes a very great difference, or rather *all* the difference', he insisted.[4]

The implication of this for governance, in Aristotle, is that the best state is one in which the young are raised from an early age to understand the complexities of moral behaviour. Morality can only exist in any useful sense if it is woven into the very fabric of the life of the state. Our contemporary idea of the ethics 'expert' who boasts specialized knowledge and strategies that can be applied like the techniques of cosmetic surgery to morally problematic situations is not one of which Aristotle would have approved. Nor would he have looked favourably on the Rationalist notion that moral outcomes can automatically be generated by institutions whose optimal performance depends on fundamentally vicious, self-interested, behaviour by individuals.

In Aristotle we are introduced to the idea that good can be more than an abstract perfection, a benchmark – that good is also what is good *for us*. Virtue is its own reward, certainly, but, in Aristotle, the virtuous person is also a happy person. As we saw in Chapter 6, modern research seems to support this contention that doing good is a prerequisite to doing well. In modern times we have distorted this ancient idea into the notion of 'doing well by doing good', which is taken to infer that it is possible to grow prosperous through good works. It is a phrase one sees often in the literature of corporate social responsibility, in which authors try to convince corporate managers that there is as much or more money to be made through socially responsible behaviour as there is in business as usual. Whether or not this is actually true remains a subject of hot debate in business journals, both academic and popular. But there would have been no doubt in Aristotle's mind: for him (and for his teacher, Plato), the question would be irrelevant because virtuous behaviour that is performed in the expectation of reward is not virtue at all, but at best, mere prudence.

In ancient Greece, however, there was no such thing as the cyber-corporation enjoying imitation personhood, those emergent entities that play such a significant role in our own era. We moderns may want to ask, if the outcomes that follow from prudent behaviour masquerading as virtue are indistinguishable from the outcomes of genuinely virtuous behaviour, does motive matter? If the river is cleaned up or the toxic waste safely recycled, do we care why?

In the case of the individual person, the answer to the question is certainly, yes. Virtuous motivation, continuously exercised in action, is what makes a virtuous person, and what makes a person virtuous. But in the case of the cybernetic machines we call modern business corporations, we can never hope for truly virtuous behaviour, any more than we can from our lawn mowers or automobiles or computers. In this case, fake virtue is better than nothing, is in fact an acceptable substitute.

As the following chapter will argue, we humans are so constructed that we can all imagine what a better world would look like, a world in which we exercise our will and serve our conscience by standing up for justice and freedom. If we can imagine institutions that promote human happiness and flourishing for its own sake, as an end in itself, we can build them, too. A politics that appeals to our better nature, to our better history, is possible, and can succeed, because such a politics would be, after all, a politics of realism, of everyday wisdom, of hope and charity.

NOTES

1. 1977 letter to the American Civil Liberties Union, quoted in Vaclav Smil, "Garrett James Hardin (Dallas 1915—Santa Barbara 2003)," *American Scientist* 92, no. 1 (2004): 8.
2. Garrett Hardin, "The Tragedy of the Commons," *Science* 162. no. 3859 (1968): 1243–48.
3. Hardin, "Commons," 1243–48.
4. *Entelecheia*, II, 1,1103b23-25.

Chapter 9:

The Morality within Us

1

When Garrett Hardin challenged long-standing dogma about the capitalist market and its magical invisible hand, he left unexamined classical economics' bedrock assumptions about what motivates people in their social lives. This accounts in large measure for his parable's widespread popularity — 'The Tragedy of the Commons' was taken to be ideologically sound, in fact neutral, particularly in the central supposition that individual self-interest is *the* determining feature of human nature.

This prejudice is foundational to all of the social sciences, and plays an especially important role in economic theory. To quote the classic McGraw-Hill textbook *Economics*: 'Capitalism presumes self-interest as the fundamental modus operandi for the various economic units as they express their free choices. The motive of self-interest gives direction and consistency to what might otherwise be an extremely chaotic economy'[1]. Self-interest here is not the healthy self-love that is a cornerstone of psychological and spiritual health, because this is unquantifiable. It is the material self-interest that exhibits itself in what we call, at its best, acquisitiveness, or at its worst, greed, avarice and lust – those desires that arise out of a preoccupation with the material, and which are commonly called vices. And which, thanks to Stanley Jevons' marginal utility theory, *are* quantifiable (Chapter 5).

But what if this assumption – however long-standing and deeply entrenched – is wrong? There is in fact little or no historical evidence that people naturally and habitually act on narrow self-interest in their private or public, economic, lives. Political scientist C.B. Macpherson and economic historian Karl Polanyi, both seminal figures in their fields, agree that, in Polanyi's words, 'the behaviour of man both in his primitive state and right through the course of history has been almost the opposite from that implied in this [egoistic] view'.[2] While both writers acknowledge the universality of egoistic behaviour in modern western capitalist cultures, they both conclude that 'it is only where capitalist relations of production prevail [...] that this is the necessary behaviour of all men [Macpherson]', and 'the market has been the outcome of a conscious and often violent intervention on the part of government which imposed the market organization on society for non-economic ends [Polanyi]'.[3] The egoistic behaviour assumed by rationalist thinkers to be a fact of human nature, they argue, is actually behaviour *imposed* on people living in modern market capitalist societies where it is received wisdom that 'nice guys finish last'. It is behaviour that goes against the grain, but is necessary for survival. Liberal capitalist dogma tells us that social institutions were invented as a way to productively channel incorrigibly egoistic behaviour, but the evidence points to habitual self-interest as a mode of behaviour imposed by the social institutions of market capitalism, which were developed to further the interests of the prevailing economic powers.

To mistake the reality of egoistic behaviour in market economies for 'natural law' is an error Immanuel Kant recognized as early as 1792, in an essay he called 'On the Old Saw: That May Be Right in Theory, But It Won't Work in Practice':

> One must take people as they are, our politicians tell us, and not as the world's uninformed pedants or good-natured dreamers fancy they ought to be. But *as they are* ought to read *as we have made them* by unjust coercion, by treacherous designs which the government is in a good position to carry out. In this way, the prophecy of the supposed clever statesman is fulfilled.

Philosophers, starting with Socrates, Plato, and Aristotle in Greece, and their contemporary Mencius, a leading Confucian philosopher in China, have agreed that human nature is either innately good or distinguished by a capacity to know good, and to have an instinctive affinity for it. For Socrates, this led to a famous dictum: *All wrongdoing is involuntary.* A person who chooses what is not good is doing so in the mistaken belief that it is good. No one, he said, would ever knowingly choose evil when he might choose good. Wrongdoing in this sense is involuntary. (Here we might reflect on the motive of the terrorist who believes slaughter of the innocent will lead to a higher good.)

Plato believed that the human soul partook of a numinous good, which was the fundamental reality and illumination of the universe. Aristotle observed, 'If there is some end of the things we do which we desire for its own sake, clearly this must be the good', and also, bringing this down to Earth, 'Most people would rather give than get affection'.[4] Early Christian philosophy was profoundly influenced by the Greeks, and even St. Augustine, with his notorious emphasis on original sin, conceded that there was an instinct within humans to struggle against the temptations of evil. In Protestant theology of the Enlightenment era, people are capable of distinguishing right from wrong, though only with the intervention of God's grace.[5] Modern Catholicism, since St. Thomas Aquinas (1225–74), has taken the position that humans, having been made in God's image, are innately good, and have an innate sense of right and wrong.[6]

Throughout history, in the major philosophies of East and West there has been a broad and deep consensus that moral consciousness, an innate sense of goodness, precedes moral reasoning and gives it its subject matter.

Economists and rationalist philosophers of the eighteenth and nineteenth centuries, in their determination to free themselves from the intellectual and moral strictures of Roman Catholicism, challenged the ancient idea of an innate moral impulse in people in two ways: by appealing to the experience and observations of their (mainly upper-class) readers, and disparaging earlier Aristotelian and Christian ideas on the subject. Utilitarians, for example, were fond of pointing to the dissolute and vice-ridden lives of the Victorian urban poor as evidence that people in their 'savage' state were anything but moral creatures. The fact that these well-connected and well-to-do writers themselves, like the rest of their class, were much better behaved was taken as proof of superior discipline resulting from better breeding.

The publication of Charles Darwin's *On the Origin of Species* (1859) and its theory of evolution by natural selection inflated the prestige of liberal market dogma by lending scientific legitimacy to the notion of competition and self-interest as inherited human traits, necessary to human progress. Just as life-or-death competition for food led to the natural selection of the better-adapted individuals in a species, the ruthless competition in market economies weeded out the inefficient players.

But recent psychological studies of children confirm what parents know, that there is a strong sense of right and wrong present even in toddlers. (The various skills and abilities needed to act on those instincts take longer to develop, as parents learn.) Vivian Gussin Paley, a noted researcher into childhood development, writes of the enormous empathy and respect she had observed in a group of kindergarten kids who had a disabled child in their midst: 'Walking to my hotel, a curious notion enters my mind. When God promises Abraham not to destroy the wicked cities of Sodom and Gomorrah if even ten righteous people can be found, how differently the biblical tale might have ended had Abraham searched in [this kindergarten] classroom'.[7]

Field observation and lab experiments with a wide range of non-human animal species have demonstrated that many of them also exhibit genuine altruism in a variety of circumstances. This is behaviour that is other-directed and for which there is no discoverable payback, immediate or future, either to the actor or its kin-group.[8] Rhesus monkeys will refuse food rather than administer electric shocks to cage-mates; bonobos have been observed helping wounded birds to fly; chimps will hug victims of abuse. From these and many other observations of primates, biologist Franz de Waal, for one, has concluded that 'we are moral beings to the core'.[9] Examples of altruism among non-primates from elephants to rats and bats, as well, continue to grow both in the academic literature,[10] and on YouTube, where anecdotal video evidence proliferates daily.

Nevertheless, de Waal notes, most of his fellow scientists seem perfectly happy to report some animal behaviours as 'aggressive', but reluctant to characterize other acts as altruistic, or even 'sympathetic'. When animals show undeniable tendencies to altruism or tolerance, these terms are typically placed in quotation marks, or given negative labels, as when preferential treatment of kin is called 'nepotism', rather than 'love of kin'. Given that we cannot know the thought processes of other humans, let alone other primates, this kind of reporting, while claiming to conserve objectivity, seems rather to indicate bias.

Immanuel Kant offered a helpful thought experiment in support of his contention that the moral impulse is both real and potent. He asks readers of his *Critique of Practical Reason* (1788) to imagine a man walking by one of the many brothels that were a feature of most European cities in his time. The man knows he ought not to go in, but is unable to resist the call of lust and pleasure. Now, Kant says, imagine that a gallows has been erected outside the brothel promising certain death to all who enter. Will the man then be able to resist temptation? Of course he will: his desire for life is far stronger than all other animal passions. And now imagine that the same man is commanded by his ruler, on pain of hanging, to sign a document falsely accusing an innocent person of an offence punishable by death. The subject of this experiment, we can safely assume, will hesitate, uncertain as to what to do. Nor would any of the rest of us be sure, given the same circumstances. None of us can be certain that we would do the right thing in the face of death (though history and experience tell us that some of us undoubtedly would). It is in that moment of indecision, Kant says, that we experience our freedom, our ability to triumph over our baser instincts. We also, importantly, demonstrate our knowledge that there is a *right* thing to do.

It is also in this moment of indecision that we demonstrate the potential for ideas to alter the course of events in the physical universe, even against the heaviest of odds. Plato has a simple, and perhaps even more telling experiment: ask yourself, would you rather do evil and be regarded as good, or do good and be thought of as evil? Try it: most of us are at least ambivalent. And it is in our knowing what is right that we demonstrate the existence of moral reality, or, we might say, the existence of *moral fact*.

2

But the big question remains: If people have an innate moral sense, where does it come from? Noam Chomsky, one of the twentieth century's most influential scientists and philosophers, was among the first to offer a coherent answer. In a tour de force of combined observation and theory Chomsky, early in his career, challenged the behaviourist belief that children learn to speak simply by being taught, pointing to evidence showing that infants are hard-wired with an innate linguistic grammar that makes it possible for them to learn languages. If this were not the case, he was able to demonstrate, they would not be able to become fluent nearly as quickly as they do, if at all.

This realization led Chomsky to speculate that other 'grammars' might well be part of human inheritance at birth: 'The evidence seems compelling, indeed overwhelming, that fundamental aspects of our mental and social life [...] are determined as part of our biological endowment, not acquired by learning, still less by training, in the course of our experience'. Next to language, the most probable candidate for such unconscious, innate knowledge seemed to Chomsky to be morality:

The acquisition of a specific moral and ethical system, wide ranging and often precise in its consequences, cannot simply be the result of 'shaping' and 'control' by the social environment. As in the case of language, the environment is far too impoverished and indeterminate to provide this system to the child, in its full richness and applicability. Knowing little about the matter, we are compelled to speculate; but it certainly seems reasonable to speculate that the moral and ethical system acquired by the child owes much to some innate human faculty. The environment is relevant, as in the case of language, vision, and so on; thus we can find individual and cultural divergence. But there is surely a common basis, rooted in our nature.[11]

The political philosopher and ethical theorist John Rawls arrived at a similar conclusion in puzzling over the roots of morality. He noted, as Chomsky had, the surprising and apparently innate ability we have as young children to recognize and create well-formed sentences, a basic ability which we build on through instruction and experience. And he wrote that moral concepts such as our sense of justice, evident from a very early age, would appear to be constructed on a similar foundation, on an innate, universal *moral* grammar. As with basic linguistic ability, this grammar is common to all people, but it is expressed differently in different cultures. In the same way as English, Japanese, Arabic and Urdu are culturally shaped expressions of a basic linguistic ability among humankind, what we call moral relativism amounts to cultural variations on a foundational moral grammar that we all share. Rawls insists that '[t]here is no reason to assume that our sense of justice can be adequately characterized by familiar common-sense precepts, or derived from the more obvious learning principles'. Our moral capacities 'go beyond the norms and standards cited in everyday life'.[12]

As Chomsky says:

Why does everyone take for granted that we don't learn to grow arms, but rather, are designed to grow arms? Similarly, we should conclude that in the case of the development of moral systems, there's a biological endowment which in effect requires us to develop a system of moral judgment and a theory of justice, if you like, that in fact has detailed applicability over an enormous range.[13]

If it is the case that our moral behaviour is based on an innate grammar, or disposition, or proclivity, it should be possible to demonstrate this in formal psychological experiments. Remarkably, research into the roots of our abilities to make moral judgements is still in its early stages but the evidence leans heavily in the direction of Rawls and Chomsky and there is little reason to expect that trend to change.[14]

The main contrary argument, frequently heard, is that the existence of widespread depravity in the world must mean that there is no such thing as an innate moral sense. It can be easily disposed of by stating the obvious: we sometimes, all of us, do things that we know are wrong to do. What is significant, and what remains mysterious is this: why do we *know* they're wrong?

NOTES

1. Paul Samuelson, *Economics* 16th ed. (New York: Irwin McGraw-Hill, 2004).

2. Karl Polanyi, *The Great Transformation* (Boston: Beacon Press, 2001 [1944]), 258.

3. C. B. Macpherson, *The Rise and Fall of Economic Justice* (Oxford: Oxford University Press, 1985), 89; Polanyi, *The Great Transformation*, 258.

4. Aristotle, *Nicomachean Ethics* (ca. 325 BCE).

5. However, because of original sin (Adam and Eve's disobedience in the Garden of Eden) humans have an inherited character flaw that leads them too often to choose wrong over right. They are thus in need of guidance.

6. However, because of original sin (Adam and Eve's disobedience in the Garden of Eden) humans have an inherited character flaw that leads them too often to choose wrong over right.

7. Quoted in Susan Neiman, *Moral Clarity* (New York: Harcourt Inc., 2008), 276.

8. Hauser, *Moral Minds*.

9. Frans de Waal, *Good Natured: The Origins of Right and Wrong in Humans and Other Animals* (Cambridge: Harvard University Press, 1996).

10. See, for example, Marc Bekoff and Jessica Pierce, *Wild Justice: The Moral Lives of Animals* (Chicago: University of Chicago Press, 2009).

11. Noam Chomsky, *Language and the Problems of Knowledge* (Cambridge: MIT Press, 1988), 161, 152.

12. John Rawls, *A Theory of Justice* (Cambridge: Harvard University Press, 1971), 47.

13. Quoted in Hauser, *Moral Minds*, x.

14. For a comprehensive survey and analysis of this research see Hauser, *Moral Minds*.

Chapter 10:

Disenchantment

1

The Enlightenment is sometimes spoken of as an era of disenchantment. This is usually, and justifiably, understood in a positive way as reason's triumph in ridding peoples' minds of baseless fears and superstitions. But there is another, less positive, sense in which the disenchantment refers to the era's leading thinkers' arbitrary repudiation of age-old ways of knowing the world that may be 'unscientific', but nevertheless can point to profound truths. For a variety of reasons, in recent decades there has been a revival of interest in sources of knowledge about humanity and the world that have been off-limits to science as traditionally practised, but nevertheless appear to be real and valuable. The status awarded to leading thinkers like Chomsky, Rawls, Nagel, Polanyi and Taylor exemplifies this fact. Today, such commonplace mysteries as the apparent existence of an innate moral grammar and its relationship to agency, values and meaning are accepted as legitimate, mainstream areas of enquiry despite the fact that they resist being reduced to the formulaic, deterministic worlds of biology or chemistry.

Moral realism has returned to respectability.

Historians will someday want to look back over the evidence and trace the origins of this welcome development. Those who are adept at spotting cycles in human affairs will point out that it coincides with a revival of the almost-forgotten philosophy of Henri Bergson (1849–1941), whose epic, early-twentieth-century confrontation with Albert Einstein pitted an intuitively sensible, realist metaphysics against Einstein's radically disruptive view of the relativity of time and space. Bergson, a buttoned-down French philosopher of austere demeanour, a Nobel laureate in literature, enjoyed an enormous celebrity in his prime and attracted huge, traffic-snarling crowds to lectures in New York City and Paris. The younger Einstein, ill-kempt German mathematical theoretician, enjoyed an equally large and improbable celebrity, a media darling who shared front-page coverage with the likes of that raffish Italian heart-throb, Guglielmo Marconi, inventor of radio. Their public sparring-match and its lopsided outcome would play an important role in defining subsequent generations' attitudes to science, technology and progress.

As a theoretical physicist, Einstein explicitly aligned himself with the position taken by Galileo at the dawning of the scientific era, that scientific, mathematical representations of the world were not simply useful models of reality, but complete and accurate representations of reality itself. In Einstein's physics, time exists only as a theoretical concept, to be calculated in discrete units relative to the absolute speed of light. As an everyday, subjective, richly variegated human experience, time, Einstein insisted, was nothing more than a psychological quirk. It followed that in studying the nature of time as it is experienced in life, philosophers (such as Bergson) were concerning themselves with something that 'has no existence'. By implication, then, neither did much else that humans experience as central to their very being, the intangible *qualities* of things as opposed to their (measurable) quantities.

Bergson's metaphysics, on the other hand, attributed the most fundamental level of human knowing, which he called 'intuition', to the experience shared by all living things of being embedded in the episodic, unpredictable lifeworld of the phenomenon of time – or as he preferred to call it, duration (*la durée*). He defined intuition as the direct, organic knowledge gained from this rich experience and which provided the foundation for the kind of human intelligence used to construct the useful abstractions science and mathematics use to describe things – the kind of 'surface knowledge' on exhibit in Einstein's theories. Human experience, life as lived through time, in other words, was *anything but* an illusory psychological response to the objective physical 'reality' described in Einstein's theoretical physics. The opposite was the case.

The public's growing interest in scientific and technological novelty fed by war and its machinery; the weary post-war relativism and cynicism of much of European political and philosophical thought; Einstein's carefully groomed public profile and the tidy, value-neutral nature of his physics *vis a vis* Bergson's complex morally portentous metaphysics all fit the zeitgeist of the time and conspired to deliver a crushing defeat to Bergson and his philosopher allies, from which his ideas are only now beginning to recover.[1]

2

The resurgence of interest in alternatives to hard-core physics as a comprehensive representation of reality got a jolt of energy in 1929, with the publication by astronomer Edwin Hubble of conclusive evidence that the universe is finite, expanding and had a beginning at a definite point in time about twenty billion years ago. This revelation came as an enormous shock to a generation of astronomers, cosmologists and physicists (including Einstein) who had accepted the previous, more comfortable consensus of a steady-state universe that had no beginning and no ending. It forced them to consider questions that their training had not equipped them to answer, such as: if the universe had a beginning, what caused it to begin? Was the universe created out of nothing, *ex nihilo*? Or did something come before?

The difficulty was that, in the initiating event that science has dubbed the Big Bang, the extreme temperature and pressure had made it impossible for physical evidence of what might have come before to have survived. The universe was born under conditions in which our laws of physics do not apply. It is a product of circumstances we can never know.

Another, even more troublesome set of questions raised by the Big Bang involve direction, or telos: the universe is evolving from a defined staring point, but in what direction? Towards what end? If it has a beginning and is evolving, does it also have meaning? How might this be influencing humanity?

As astronomer Robert Jastrow writes, 'A sound explanation may exist for the explosive birth of our universe, but if it does, science cannot find out what the explanation is. The scientist's pursuit of the past ends in the moment of creation'. In other words, science has been confronted with precisely that which Rationalists insisted did not exist: 'a natural occurrence which cannot be explained, even with unlimited time and money' – and not just any natural occurrence, but the most fundamental of all. As Jastrow says, 'for the scientist who has lived by his faith in the power of reason', the story of the past four hundred years of scientific discovery 'ends like a bad dream. He has scaled the mountains of ignorance; he is about to conquer the highest peak; as he pulls himself over the final rock, he is greeted by a band of theologians who have been sitting there for centuries'.[2] Among them, presumably, St. Augustine, who on contemplating Genesis ('In the beginning God created heaven and earth [...]') remarked, 'Who can understand this mystery or explain it to others?'[3]

Or perhaps our growing distrust of science's claims to exclusive access to reliable knowledge began with mathematician Kurt Gödel's famous incompleteness theorems, which demonstrate with absolute certainty that there can never be a complete, consistent, mathematical (and therefore, strictly speaking, scientific) description of reality. Gödel announced in 1931 that any moderately complex system of axioms (i.e. equations describing a theory) will generate questions that, though valid and answerable, can be neither proved nor disproved. This is a property of formal systems in general – that is, it applies to any rule-based model of a theory based in abstract thought. A comprehensive mathematical representation of reality, such as proposed by Galileo and, later, by Einstein, is such a formal system. Suppose you had what you believed was a totally complete dictionary; all the words in it must, of course, be defined using other words in that same dictionary. Suppose you then discovered a word that did not exist in the dictionary – there would be no way to define it, though it had a definition; no way to know what it meant, though it had meaning. You could create a new, expanded dictionary to include it, but that dictionary, too, would be open to the same problem – and on and on. With any formal mathematical system, Gödel discovered, there will always be loose ends like that. The remarkable, unavoidable, takeaway is that theoretical physics, a formal system described in mathematics, cannot, in *principle*, provide a complete picture of our world. There will always be knowledge that exists outside its purview. It will always be incomplete.

Quantum physics pioneer Werner Heisenberg's uncertainty principle (1927) similarly casts doubt on the ability of physics to draw a complete picture of the world: it demonstrates that it is in principle impossible to know everything there is to know about quantum particles at any given time. For example, either position or momentum can be measured and recorded, but not both.

If experimental confirmation of theories proves to be impossible, two ways remain to judge one against another: by aesthetic appeal, which is largely subjective; or by conformity to some higher standard of truth, which science has traditionally insisted does not exist. The latter is Jastrow's nightmare scenario.

2

Theoretical physics has had to confront other limits in recent years. Physicists themselves agree that while quantum theory in its latest iterations fits with experimental evidence from Europe's hadron collider and other labs, it is also literally 'incomprehensible' beyond the esoteric realm of pure mathematics. Harvard physicist Sheldon Gashow, a Nobel Prize winner for contributions to quantum theory, notes that current, advanced ideas such as superstring theory are 'far beyond any empirical test'. These theories are so far into mathematical abstraction and so far beyond any possible experimental confirmation that, 'for the first time since the Dark Ages [*sic*], we can see how our noble search may end, with faith replacing science once again'.[4]

Physicists John Wheeler and David Bohm, among others, have argued that quantum theory clearly indicates that reality is not entirely physical, since it is predicated on the involvement of a conscious observer: quanta exist only as statistical probabilities until they are observed, at which time they become either existent or non-existent.[5] The world is, in a real sense, manufactured by consciousness. Perhaps there is an 'implicate, objective order' underlying it all as Bohm asserts, but if there is, it is 'unknown and cannot be grasped by thought'. ('Implicate', a rare and lovely adjective, means *folded in*.) Bohm has expressed the hope that, in future, science will be 'less dependent on mathematics for modeling reality and [will] draw on new sources of metaphor and analogy' such as art.[6]

Or perhaps disillusionment with scientific certainty came with the failure of artificial intelligence (AI) research to bear out the rationalist supposition that the brain is a machine, the functioning of which can be reduced to algorithms and replicated in other machines. The notion that thought is a kind of computation reaches back to Hobbes: 'By *ratiocination*, I mean *computation*', he proclaimed (in 1656). Thinking, he said, is like speaking or writing in that involves the manipulation of symbols (words that represent things), but since it is internal, it uses special brain tokens he called 'phantasms' or thought 'parcels'. The manipulating of those parcels, if it were to produce sound results, had to take place within strict rules of reason – what we might now call algorithms.[7] Where the rules of symbol manipulation are bent, thinking is flawed.

That other icon of Modernity, René Descartes (1596–1650), proposed that mind and matter were separate substances. 'I think therefore I am' (the famous Cartesian *cogito*) he took to be the irreducible baseline of human knowledge, a truth about his own existence that cannot be denied. Since, for Descartes, mind and body were different kinds of substances, mind could in principle exist without a material embodiment. Out of this arose the notorious mind-body problem: how, exactly, do the two interact? What's the causal connection that allows the mind to move the body?

AI research was confidently undertaken in the aftermath of Second World War in the joint Hobbesean–Cartesian assumption that the human brain was essentially a more complex version of the newly invented electronic digital computer, which is an algorithm-based symbol-manipulator *par excellence*. Indeed, the standard criterion proposed for machine intelligence was the so-called 'Turing test'[8] in which a person in one room communicates with a computer and with another person, both hidden in a second room, asking questions of both. (Turing had them chat via teleprinter.) If the person in the first room is unable to tell which of his communicants is a computer and which a person, the computer is deemed to be intelligent. This, of course, repeats Francis Bacon's seventeenth-century fallacy that scientific descriptions that 'save all the appearances' are the same as definitive explanations. In other words, a map and the territory it describes are essentially identical, or in this case, an exact imitation is qualitatively the same as the original. More specifically, it can be said that unlike the computational processes of computers, human thinking involves more than just syntax – the rule-based manipulation of symbols – it also concerns itself with semantics; thoughts have aboutness – they *refer* to something.

John Haugeland (1945–2010), a philosopher specializing in philosophy of mind and cognitive science, wrote of what he called 'the paradox of mechanical reason'. He defined reasoning in AI terms as 'the manipulation of meaningful symbols according to rational rules'. Noting that, by definition, there needs to be some sort of manipulator involved, he continued:

There seems to be two basic possibilities: whether the manipulator pays attention to what the symbols and rules *mean* or it doesn't. If it pays attention to the meanings, then it can't be entirely mechanical – because meanings (whatever exactly they are) don't exert physical forces.

But if the manipulator doesn't pay attention to the meanings 'then the manipulations can't be instances of reasoning – because what's reasonable or not depends crucially on what the symbols mean'. In other words, if it's a machine it can't reason; if it can reason it can't be a machine. This is in effect a paraphrase of philosopher John Searle's famous thought experiment, 'the Chinese room' (1980).[9] Both arguments appear to show conclusively that what was called 'strong AI' – the notion that an appropriately programmed computer of sufficient power could have a mind in exactly the same sense as humans have minds – is impossible.

In any case, AI achieved none of its initial objectives in terms of either explaining how the brain works or creating intelligence in a machine. Even the much-ballyhooed chess tournaments between grand master Gary Kasparov and IBM's Deep Blue computer (1996–97) served only to highlight the failure. Kasparov won the first tournament, and his narrow loss in the rematch was contested and remains controversial. Science journalist John Horgan commented:

> Chess, with its straightforward rules and tiny Cartesian playing field, is a game tailor-made for computers. And Deep Blue, whose five handlers include the best chess programmers in the world, is a prodigiously powerful machine, with 32 parallel processors capable of examining 200 million positions each second. If this silicon monster cannot defeat a mere human at chess, what hope is there that computers will ever mimic our more subtle talents [...].[10]

More recently, scientists have begun programming computers to sift through vast databases in an iterative learning process in which software bootstraps itself into steadily growing levels of knowledge and, presumably, intelligence. But a leading researcher, Jaron Lanier, has noted of these forays into 'machine learning' through evolution:

> There has now been a decade of work world-wide in Darwinian approaches to generating software, and while there have been some fascinating and impressive isolated results, and indeed I enjoy participating in such research, nothing has arisen from the work that would make software in general any better [...] So, while I love Darwin, I won't count on him to write code.[11]

It's important to note that AI research can be divided into two broad categories: cognitive artificial intelligence and applied artificial intelligence. Progress in applied AI has been brilliant: computers can play world-beating chess, diagnose diseases, build automobiles, analyse written texts, make sense of complex databases, operate household appliances and military weapons systems, and almost anything else that we humans do by consciously or even unconsciously following rules (algorithms) of one kind or another. Progress in cognitive AI, in teaching computers to be creative, to conceive analogies and metaphors, to exhibit ordinary, everyday common sense ingenuity and insight, to literally think outside the box, has, however, been less than stellar.

When it comes to applied AI, today's supercomputers make Deep Blue look primitive, and quantum computing is on the horizon. But the fact remains that machine intelligence, however generated, can never be more than exactly that: *machine* intelligence. It cannot duplicate human intelligence or 'surpass' human cognitive abilities for the simple reason that our cognition is embodied. It is, in other words, an evolutionary feature of a particular kind of living creature, in which it exists not just in neuronal processes in the brain (itself shaped by experience), but distributed throughout the body. The human environment and the nature of the sensory apparatus through which we experience it are foundational to our intelligence. What we call 'muscle memory' is an expression of embodiment, and when even ordinary, everyday memories arise, it is often impossible to separate intellectual, emotional, chemical and muscular components.

Or think of it this way: we know that cognition and emotion are not separate kinds of thinking; they are intimately entwined and occur simultaneously. Cognitive scientist and early AI researcher Marvin Minsky noted in his landmark *The Society of Mind* (1986): 'Our culture wrongly teaches us that thoughts and feelings lie in almost two separate worlds. In fact, they're always intertwined'. The psychologist R.B. Zajpnic wrote, in a similar vein '[…] in nearly all cases […] feeling is not free of thought, nor is thought free of feeling'.[12] And psychologist Howard Leventhal writes that 'emotion itself is a form of cognition'.[13] This poses an obvious problem for the development of cognitive AI, since machines do not, and cannot, have emotions – certainly not *human* emotions. And it follows that if human thought almost always contains an emotional component as well as a cognitive component, and is shaped by their interaction, then the hurdles facing this area of research are very high indeed.

Moreover, human intelligence is deeply influenced by culture, both prehistoric and current, to the degree that it makes little sense to speak of the individual human intellect without acknowledging that connection. As David Bohm writes, human thought is, in an important sense, collective: '[...] most of our thought in its general form is not individual. It originates in the whole culture and pervades us [...]. This deep structure of thought, which is the source, the constant source – timeless – is always there'.[14] Moral knowledge, which is implicit in humans (and perhaps other species as well), would appear to belong in this 'deep structure' category.

And related to this is what Michael Polanyi calls 'tacit knowledge', skills, ideas and intuitions that we possess, knowingly or otherwise, but cannot easily express in words.[15] It is knowledge that comes with lived experience, freighted with emotion. It is why 'book learning' is no substitute for 'hands-on' experience, and why we apprentice with experts; to extract such knowledge from another person often requires close contact over time, as in a mentorship. It is why we can instantly recognize our child's face among hundreds of others. It is what enables us to derive meaning from language. Riding a bicycle, driving a car, or playing a musical instrument, or building fine cabinetry, or diagnosing obscure illnesses, or writing fine poetry, or developing elegant scientific hypotheses are all examples from daily life where tacit knowledge is essential. Polanyi believed that all living organisms possess some degree of tacit knowledge of the world around them, enabling them to survive. A great deal of what we know consists of this kind of knowledge, much of it all but impossible to put into words: as Polanyi says, 'We know more than we can tell'.[16] The depth and complexity of the deep structure of knowledge – of tacit knowledge – plus the fact that we are in most cases unable to express it in explicit terms mean that it is all but impossible to translate it into the language of computers.

For Polanyi, the accumulation of tacit knowledge is a process common to all living things, and has been going on since life emerged. It has shaped evolution of species individually and collectively. In humans it is a large part of what accounts for selfhood, the individual and unique 'me'.

The idea of thought and knowledge as embodied can seem counterintuitive, because it turns an important aspect of rationalist culture, and current conventional wisdom, on its head. Descartes' mind-body dualism, with mind being a separate, non-material substance – the 'ghost in the machine' as the behaviourist Gilbert Ryle scoffed[17] – is replaced by the idea that thought, or mind, emerges organically as the physical body interacts with its environment. To conceptually separate mind and body, as Descartes did, is to misunderstand the essence of thought as inescapably the product of a material process. It is not so much that mind ought to be placed in the category of the 'material', but to acknowledge, with current quantum science, that the material is 'not just mechanical'.[18] There is more to matter than meets the eye; mind and matter seem to be 'entangled' in a way that is analogous to the fact/value relationship discussed earlier.[19]

3

While AI researchers were busily modelling the brain as a series of electronic circuits, neurophysiologists were uncovering in their research into neuroplasticity a far more exciting reality – namely that the human brain is capable of altering its own physical structure through thought. Stroke victims, for example, can repair damaged brain functions through determined and repetitive mental effort which reconstitutes lost capabilities by physically changing the brain. And musicians and meditators have been shown to have the ability to change their own brain activity and, in time, brain structure, through sheer imagination. The *brain states* that cause clinical depression through various neurochemical processes can be altered by improving the patient's *mind state*.

We have long understood that we are what we eat; we now have solid evidence that we are what we think, as well.[20] We have always known that the mind is able to create 'virtual' objects and happenings that do not exist in the realm of 'material' reality; we are now able to demonstrate that those imagined objects and happenings are themselves real in some important delimiting sense, because they are capable of causing change in the physical world.

The mystery that needs to be solved is not how and why the mind is able to act on the physical world (enabling me, for example, to type this sentence as I create it in thought), but how and why and to what degree mind and body are ultimately of the same substance, each permeating the other, so that, in physics, the presence of a conscious observer can determine whether or not a sub-atomic particle exists or remains only a potential.

The closest we've come to a scientific answer is in the study of complexity and emergence theory, the hypothesis that complex systems can, and often do, spontaneously produce emergent properties capable of reaching back into the system and altering it (Chapter 7). But this is an observation, not an explanation. As the philosopher Thomas Nagel points out, emergence theory can make sense only if there are some pre-existing physical characteristics in what we think of as the material world, which give rise to consciousness. That is:

> [T]he propensity for the development of organisms with a subjective point of view [i.e., a mind] must have been there from the beginning, just as the propensity for the formation of atoms, molecules, galaxies, and organic compounds must have been there from the beginning, in consequence of the already existing properties of the fundamental particles.[21]

It may be that these are unanswerable questions. There seem to be aspects of existence so fundamental, so elemental, that they cannot be described in terms of other features of life and nature, or even in terms of the phenomena they generate. In other words, as the sciences expand their horizons of understanding, at some stage the realities they become aware of may no longer be concrete and specific, but radically basic and transcendent, and therefore opaque to our finite minds, like David Bohm's undiscoverable 'implicate order'. Only observation from outside can yield conclusive knowledge about a contained or bounded formal system, and science itself has demonstrated to its own satisfaction that at some level of theoretical enquiry, even in so large a system as the universe, we inevitably run up against definitive boundaries beyond which reason has no power to penetrate. When we reach them, we can only turn inward, calling on intuition, imagination and the language of metaphor to explain the inexplicable. The things we cannot explain, we can only acknowledge, based on the everyday evidence of their existence, and provide with names of our own invention: 'life', 'consciousness', 'love', 'good', 'gravity'.

Given the truism that our biggest problems are caused, not by lack of knowledge, but by believing in false knowledge (as the rationalists did), this new attitude of epistemic humility can only be welcome.

NOTES

1. The Einstein–Bergson dispute is detailed comprehensively in Jimena Canales, *The Physicist and the Philosopher: Einstein, Bergson, and the Debate that Changed Our Understanding of Time* (Princeton: Princeton University Press, 2015). See also John Mullarkey, ed., *The New Bergson* (Manchester: Manchester University Press, 1999), and David Lapoujade, *Powers of Time: Versions of Bergson*, trans. Andrew Goffey (Minneapolis: University of Minnesota Press, 2018).

2. Robert Jastrow, *God and the Astronomers* (New York: W.W. Norton, 1978).

3. *Confessions* 11.9. This is a rough paraphrase of Augustine's elaborate prose: 'In this Beginning, O God, hast Thou made heaven and earth, in Thy Word, in Thy Son, in Thy Power, in Thy Wisdom, in Thy Truth; wondrously speaking, and wondrously making. Who shall comprehend? Who declare it? ...'

4. Quoted in John Horgan, *The End of Science: Facing the Limits of Knowledge in the Twilight of the Scientific Age* (London: Abacus, 2007), 63.

5. The idea is startlingly similar to Aristotle's notion of a reality that exists *in potentia*, to be brought into existence through interaction with the mind.

6. Horgan, *The End of Science*, 88.

7. By this definition both thought and language are formal systems.

8. Proposed by Alan Turing, mathematician, logician and inventor of the general-purposed electronic computer. An effective critique is provided by John Searle.

9. Searle, 'Chinese room' thought experiment, "Minds, Brains and Programs," in *Behavioral and Brain Sciences* 3, no. 3 (1980): 417–457.

10. John Horgan, "Deep Blue Team Plots Its Next Move," 1996.

11. Jaron Lanier, "One Half of a Manifesto" (NY: Union Square Press, 2008), 330.

12. Quoted in David Gelernter, *The Muse in the Machine: Computerizing the Poetry of Human Thought* (New York: Free Press/Macmillan, 1994), 43.

13. Gelernter, *The Muse in the Machine*, 43.

14. David Bohm, *On Dialogue* (New York: Routledge, 1996), 59.

15. Michael Polanyi, *The Tacit Dimension* (Chicago: University of Chicago Press, 1966), 4. Polanyi, a scientist and philosopher whose achievements are so wide-ranging as to resist categorization, is usually described in biographies as a polymath.

16. Michael Polanyi, *Knowing and Being* (London: Routledge and Kegan Paul, 1966), 133. Note the obvious parallels with Henri Bergson's notion of intuition as opposed to intelligence touched on above.

17. Gilbert Ryle, *The Concept of Mind* (Chicago: University of Chicago Press, 1949).

18. Bohm, *On Dialogue*.

19. A comprehensive introduction to the philosophy of mind is George Graham's *Philosophy of Mind: An Introduction* (Malden: Blackwell, 2002).

20. For a highly accessible survey of the science of neuroplasticity, see Norman Doidge, *The Brain That Changes Itself* (New York: Penguin Books, 2007).

21. Thomas Nagel, *Mind and Cosmos* (Oxford University Press, 2012), 61. Nagel is a leading contemporary proponent of the idea of 'panpsychism', a form of reductionism arguing that the material and mental co-exist in everything.

Chapter 11:

The Ultimate Technology: Trans-Humanism and Post-Humanism

1

It is certainly true that the world is more complicated than it used to be, in part because, while the power of technology solves many problems, it magnifies others and creates unexpected challenges in the form of unintended consequences. Smart phones and social media are current examples that readily come to mind. But it is also true that while the fundamental issues facing us are different in scale from those facing our ancestors, they are similar in kind. Our goal remains to live a good life, to do what we can to help others do the same, and to respect the natural systems that make life possible, so that they can be passed on to succeeding generations in a healthy state. I have argued that how we achieve these timeless goals is not a question primarily for experts or technicians or 'specialists', but for ordinary people of adequate education who have some time for reflection in their lives, and who have the means to engage in civil discourse. The really important issues facing us, the inconvenient truths we can no longer avoid, are not technical, but moral. And as Plato said, and modern moral realists agree, we are all experts in morality.

Beginning with the Enlightenment-era's noble, if rash, determination to free humanity from the 'yoke' of religion and other forms of irrational, metaphysical speculation, western civilization has proceeded through a series of well-meaning humanistic, scientistic, enterprises that risked throwing the baby out with the bathwater. Everything from large-scale utilitarian social engineering (market capitalism and its trappings) to consumer culture and advanced corporate management techniques, ultimately onward to current bioengineering projects, aimed at producing technologically enhanced human beings who will presumably be better equipped to cope with the world as we have left it. Also on offer these days are super-intelligent computers, perhaps encased in articulated robotic bodies, that will outstrip human capabilities in every respect and will be capable of colonizing Mars and perhaps other nearby planets. 'To what possible end?' is a question that can only be answered, if at all, with historical context.

2

Humanity's love affair with technology really gets underway with the industrial revolution of the late eighteenth century, beginning in Britain and spreading through Europe before crossing the Atlantic. Machines powered by steam, and later by internal combustion engines and electricity, increased by orders of magnitude our ability to manipulate the natural environment, extract resources, and transport goods and materials. Scientific discoveries were for the first time systematically being transformed into technologies by a new actor on the stage – the professional engineer – who specialized in maximizing the efficient use of resources in production processes.

Since a key resource in industrial processes was labour, by the late nineteenth century engineers were being called upon to turn their talents to the design of systems for managing workers and employees. The earliest university-level management training schools were staffed by professional engineers, who saw human labour as a resource amenable to carefully managed exploitation in pursuit of the efficiencies that come with standardization of inputs and the efficient substitution it allows.[1]

The object was to transform labour relations from the employment of unruly, independent, human beings to the management of uniform, compliant, *human resources*. Standardization, and with it, easy substitution of inputs, was to be achieved through public school systems teaching standard curricula, vocational schools, and factory training programs. As Frederick W. Taylor wrote in his classic *Shop Management* (1911), the object was to remove the irrational and the emotional aspects of human participation in organizational life, replacing it with formal, rationalistic structures that would ensure maximum efficiency and minimal conflict. 'All possible brain work should be removed from the shop and centered in the planning department', he said. The ideal production line employee would be functionally indistinguishable from a robot.

Erwin Schell, a mechanical engineer by training and an early dean of what would become the Sloan School of Management at MIT, wrote about the professional manager's mission in a 1913 lecture called 'The Workmen: Their Impulses and Desires'. In it, he discusses how workers' motivations can be reduced to a few basic impulses, and how a skilled manager might use them to advantage.

> The executive who, by facilitating promotion [...] makes marriage a possibility for a young man (thereby dealing with the 'Sex Impulse') stands to receive large dividends in increased loyalty and length of service [...]. The executive who assigns the new employee a locker, a key, a machine and bench, with name affixed, is bringing instinctive satisfactions to proprietorship ('the Wish to Possess') which show returns in reduced turnover [...]. The Desire for Leadership is sometimes called the submissive impulse. I like to think of it, however, as the desire to work under good leadership [...].

Thus begins the engineering interest in manipulability of human nature. It took two forms, both concerned with the problem of 'industrial waste and inefficiency' resulting from churn in the labour force caused by accidents, poor morale, and inadequate training. The 'industrial relations' approach aimed at improving the lot of workers in order to gain their cooperation and loyalty. The goal was to adjust industrial conditions to better reflect the needs of workers in response to radical criticisms of capitalism and the rising power of organized labour, following the Bolshevik revolution in Russia. At the other pole was 'personnel management', so named because it aspired to employ new tools offered by modern psychology and sociology to mould, or engineer, human behaviour to conform to industrial conditions. The two systems shared a perspective on the worker as the object of scientific study and control, imposing on the workforce paradigms of industrial management traditionally applied to non-human factors of production. In the end, it would lead to the wholesale replacement of human labour with robots, beginning in the mid-twentieth century.

3

These various industrial efficiencies were so effective in increasing the supply of goods and services that they created an urgent, reciprocal need to boost consumption in order to absorb a market-clogging excess. Thus, it was during these same years of engineering's first forays into management that the advertising industry initiated its intimate relationship with Sigmund Freud, the behaviourist Ivan Pavlov, and other pioneering psychologists. The goal was to identify and exploit human frailties and insecurities in the cause of an emerging culture of consumerism. By promoting a radical version of liberalism in which the individual's needs and desires are prioritized above all else, and through the very scale of its operations, consumer advertising was able to successfully erode traditional values such as patience, thrift, modesty and moderation, cultivating instead what soon became the dominant, materialist ethos of envy, acquisitiveness, self-indulgence and extravagance. Marketers pitched as 'a new logic of living', in which individual liberty was achieved through consumer choice. Buying on credit, otherwise known as amassing debt, was pitched as 'enforced saving'; a traditional moral hazard was, through the market's sleight-of-hand, magically transformed into a virtuous practice.[2] In the *Annals of the American Academy of Political and Economic Science* for 1922, advertising was celebrated as 'an instrument of social manipulation', whose purpose is 'the nullification of the customs of ages [...] [to] break down the barriers of individual habits [...] [it is] at once the destroyer and the creator in the process of the ever-evolving new; its constructive effort is [...] to superimpose new conceptions of individual attainment and community desire'.

But advertising and the consumer ethic it promoted were about more than the creation and satisfaction of material desires, an insight developed by philosopher Raymond Williams in his famous essay 'Advertising: The Magic System'.[3] The consumer ethic, he writes, is about the promise of a utopian world where progress is never-ending, where tomorrow will always be better than today, where choice is endless, where every emotional and material want is satisfied and where happiness prevails over unhappiness. It is clear, Williams writes, 'that we have a cultural pattern in which objects are not enough, but must be validated, if only in fantasy, by association with social and personal meanings which in a different cultural pattern might be more directly available [...]'. In short, advertising-supported consumerism is a magical system based on fetish objects, 'a highly organized and professional system of magical inducements and satisfactions, functionally very similar to magical systems in simpler societies'. It is organized along familiar rationalist lines to replace, or at least supplement, more traditional ways of addressing human needs through family and community relations, religious observances and service to others.

In the twentieth century, consumer advertising became ubiquitous, in print and outdoor displays, then on radio, and then on television, and not only as a necessary driver of continuing economic growth. It would soon become an expensive necessity for successful political campaigns as well, making more extensive political fund-raising necessary, which in turn led to new relationships of dependency with major donors, corporate and individual. Political campaigning would inevitably come to share the techniques of consumer advertising, with highly condensed messaging aimed at stirring emotional responses, the political parties framing themselves as 'brands'. Commercial sponsorship became, in America, an essential source of finance for every aspect of culture, including, crucially, the dissemination of news and information that is a cornerstone of successful democracies. (In most of the rest of the world, governments recognized the risks involved with dependency on advertising revenue, and the need for public financing of important cultural assets such as broadcasting.)

4

Interest in the malleability and manipulability of peoples' emotional, psychological and even intellectual make-up further broadened throughout the twentieth century as science, technology and engineering turned their attention to such fields as genetics, reproduction, neurology, pharmacology, medical technology, communication technology and information theory.

With the development of cybernetics by Norbert Weiner and other engineers in the war years of the 1940s, the conceptual gap between the biological and the mechanical was bridged by placing 'smart' machines and living creatures on the same plane as self-organizing, self-sustaining *cybernetic* systems. (The word is derived from the Greek for 'steersman'.) It had long been understood that a degree of self-regulation and autonomy in machines can be achieved by feedback loops, in which data about the external environment is collected and stored by the machine, which then adjusts its operations in response; that, in turn, can cause changes in the environment, completing the loop. A home heating system controlled by a thermostat is the classic example. In 1948 Claude Shannon's watershed paper 'A Mathematical Theory of Communication' provided a powerful, mechanizing adjunct to cybernetics by showing how to quantify communication of all kinds, both machine and human, by reducing it to algorithms and the manipulation of symbols, and ultimately to the manipulation of 'bits', 1's and 0's, in digital computers.[4]

In conceptualizing both mental processes and biology as technology, and vice versa, the new science of cybernetics was supplying the last pieces for the 400-year-old theoretical model of a mechanistic, deterministic world in which living entities of all kinds are essentially machines governed by algorithms, and therefore completely understandable in rational terms, reducible to material components. As the field has advanced over the past half-century, the result has been that 'machines and technological systems are becoming increasingly lifelike: [...] The warm organism and the cold mechanism are growing toward one another'.[5] Cybernetics has made possible, for better or worse, the application of industrial processes to our biological, mental and social lives. Cyborgs, part technological, part human, are moving out of the pages of science fiction novels into daily life with everything from cranial implants that regulate brain functions to prosthetic limbs that can touch and 'feel'.

In January of 1999, in the last year of the old millennium, three books were published that set the agenda for animated public conversations about what it means to be human in the age of robots, cyborgs and machine learning.[6] All three predicted a future in which humanity's flesh-and-blood-borne consciousness would be supplanted by neural networks running on silicon chips. The first and most obvious question this prediction raises is, why would we want to create such a 'post-human' future? To what end? In all three books the implied answer reaches back to Francis Bacon and the Enlightenment ethos in which technological advance is, by definition, *progress* in some normative sense. This is a belief that depends on a blind faith in science and technology that is simply not warranted by the experience of recent history. More directly to the point, a post-human world populated by machine entities would be incapable of moral behaviour rooted in an innate moral impulse, or of developing moral thought anchored in a moral sensibility, universal among humans, but necessarily absent in machines. That means that, to the extent that humanity is defined by its moral core, humanity will cease to exist. The 'post-human' turns out to be the 'sub-human'.

Again, the question must be, why pursue such a future? Beyond the technology = progress tautology, the direct answer given by computer scientist Hans Moravec and like-minded futurists is that we have no choice – the age of the intelligent machine is *inevitably* the next stage in evolution of the human species, in which we are replaced by post-human entities. Once evolution has created intelligence through natural selection, the argument goes, it is only a matter of time before intelligence creates technology. Technology then creates super-intelligence within supercomputers, and teaches it how to learn independently, and the logical next step is for the super-intelligence to supplant (or enslave) humanity entirely. This is scientific determinism taken to an absurd, even obscene, extreme.

YouTube videos excitedly show robots navigating their environment and doing human-like chores, but as we saw in the preceding chapter, it is a mistake to think that a machine capable of duplicating a human's activities in the world would necessarily be of equivalent intelligence. It is an even bigger mistake to assume that such a machine will be conscious. Even if we leave aside the issues of motivation and intentionality, we can simply assert that a human's external behaviour is far from being a complete representation of his or her inner consciousness or inner, subjective being – a fact apparently unnoticed by B.F. Skinner and other behavioural psychologists of the early twentieth century. Humans, after all, are able to pretend, to fake pain, to mimic the behaviour of others and so on. There is much more to human consciousness than is displayed in external human behaviour. The same cannot be said of robot behaviour.

Or can it? One can imagine a computer scientist proudly saying of her latest robotic creation that it 'clearly exhibits consciousness'. The problem then becomes how to prove it. We have no clear understanding of *human* consciousness, but what we do know after centuries of scientific enquiry suggests strongly that it is a manifestation of the subject's embeddedness in a biological body which in turn is the product of millions of years of evolution amid the myriad challenges presented by the Earth's environment. The idea of 'programming-in' consciousness of this kind seems frankly absurd.

Post-humanist futurism simply takes for granted that the human mind is essentially a very powerful computing machine. Information theory lends support to this idea by reducing communication, including human thought processes, to the rule-based manipulation of symbols – a process at which computers are demonstrably very good. The fact that computers may at some time in the future exceed the capacity of the human brain in the number of computations carried out per second does not mean, however, that such a computer will be a more powerful mind. The human mind does manipulate symbols, but it also does much more: human minds incorporate (or exhibit) consciousness, which remains mysterious.

Some computer scientists have proposed that consciousness, whatever else it may be, is an emergent property of the complex system that is the human brain, and that therefore the spontaneous emergence of consciousness in machines is only a matter of time, a matter of their reaching the same threshold level of complexity in their computational abilities. But a careful reading of emergence theory shows that whatever property emerges from a system, it is certain to share the essential characteristics of that system. It cannot be otherwise in a material world. In which case, machine 'consciousness', should it happen, would be utterly different from that which produces human thought.

Our minds provide us with subjective, real-world experiences that are central to our lives as human beings – introspection, the excitement of discovery, the awe of mystery, the love of others, the joy of being alive. Human minds engage in the creation of the self, the unique individual capable of self-reflection and self-recognition, self-doubt and self-assurance, self-love and self-hatred, desire and intention, processes of such complexity and mystery that, again, it seems preposterous to suppose that any computer program could be designed to mimic them. And even if it could, to replicate, or mimic, is not to reproduce. The reflexive self is surely something that can only evolve naturally, organically.

The philosopher and computer scientist Joseph Weizenbaum writes in his classic *Computer Power and Human Reason* (1976): 'No other organism, and certainly no computer, can be made to confront genuine human problems in human terms. And, since the domain of human intelligence is, except for a small set of formal problems, determined by man's [sic] humanity, every other intelligence, however great, must necessarily be alien to the human domain'. It follows, he says, that even though computer-based 'expert systems' can, in principle, be used, for example, in clinical diagnoses and judicial judgments, 'since we do not have any ways of making computers wise, we ought not to give computers tasks that demand wisdom'.[7]

Any machine, electric, electronic or mechanical, if is to do what it is designed to do (if it *works*), must operate within a set of design parameters or rules of operation, which are established by its builder. Even AI programs that are designed to 'learn' from their experience (that is, to revise their own programming on the go) do so only within the framework of their original design parameters. Therefore any 'consciousness' exhibited by such a machine 'would be simply an *accompaniment* to mechanical operations which it could not affect'. [8] What a computer scientist might proclaim to be consciousness – *eureka!* – can be nothing more than *his or her (human) interpretation of that spurious accompaniment*; the consciousness resides in the interpreter.

5

The failure of post-humanism to acknowledge the embodied nature of intelligence is in direct line of descent from Descartes, and most subsequent rationalist Enlightenment thinkers for whom mind and matter were separate kinds of phenomena. Descartes' *cogito*, 'I think therefore I am', privileged thought over matter, leading to the notion that facts arrived at through reason had higher value than those derived from direct sensory involvement with messy material realities. But thanks to the twentieth-century theoretical physics and mathematics, both quintessential products of reason, we now know with some certainty that reason is necessarily an incomplete source of knowledge; that, in fact, there are truths that we know to exist, but which we also know reason cannot illuminate for us.

Several Enlightenment-era verities are undermined by this realization, including the notion of the liberal individual, a stand-alone creature governed by an immaterial mind, morally free of all concerns beyond self-interest. If, as we now believe, mind itself is an evolutionary and cultural phenomenon rather than a divine, immaterial, endowment ('the ghost in the machine'), it seems preposterous to imagine the human race as being made up of self-contained desiring machines. The doctrine of natural law which envisions the world as an elaborate clockwork mechanism in which all activity is pre-determined is similarly invalidated by today's science, from chaos theory and its insights into unpredictability, to molecular biology which is showing that at every level of activity, the world is governed not just by happenings, but by deliberate doings as well. The Enlightenment notion of progress as a linear path in which the past is inferior to the future and the present is to be impatiently endured was, if not shattered, then severely shaken by the twentieth century's experience with technological 'progress' that brought with it factory farming, global warming, cheap and efficient genocide and thermonuclear weapons.

The gravest misconception of the rationalists, central to so much of their thinking, was the notion that a kind of synthetic morality could be concocted through pure reason, making morality virtually a branch of mathematics. The undermining of the moral authority of the Roman Catholic Church in Europe, and the confusing and contradictory ethical doctrines of the many Protestant denominations that emerged from the Reformation, left a vacuum. It was clear to the leading thinkers of the time that it needed to be filled if civilization was to endure and evolve. Confident as they were in the power of their ideas, they blithely provided a substitute in the rule-following behaviour induced by societal institutions (foreshadowed in Hobbes's *Leviathan*), in particular the capitalist market economy with its built-in inducements and punishments, and its supporting judicial and regulatory framework.

The argument being made in this book is that in these and other respects the materialist, reductionist world-view was fatally flawed from the beginning by the inadequacy of its understanding of morality, and how it can best be incorporated into our public lives – our social, political and economic endeavours. Liberal capitalism and the notion of endless 'progress' through technology, as bequeathed to us via the academic scribblings of seventeenth and eighteenth century economists, have not served us well in the long term. The case has been made a number of times in the preceding chapter – here it is again, in conclusion.

6

Throughout history, both religion and philosophy have understood morality to be related to – a manifestation of – a universal good that exists as a feature of the world, either through unknown causes related to the origins of the universe or due to the nature of, or will of, a divine Creator. Both religion and philosophy, and science, too, though with some reservations, have concluded that humankind partakes of this good. It does so either as having been created 'in God's image' or by virtue of being an evolutionary product of all of the basic components of the universe. The result in both cases is that humans (and other sentient creatures to varying degrees) share what moral realists call an innate moral sensibility, an impulse to be *for* the other.

It is on the baseline reality of this moral sense, demonstrable in history, the laboratory and in day-to-day experience, that moral realism builds its case for the existence of moral fact, or universally valid and truthful moral precepts, and adds the word 'critical' to its name.

Critical moral realism argues that the existence of this body of knowledge presents an obligation to enquire, to explore and to discuss points of convergence and divergence with others. This process leads to the creation and reinforcing of consensus, which, if it survives enough challenges over time, can be taken to be fact – though never, given human imperfections, definitively and for all time. The best we will ever be able to say is that we are as certain of 'x' as we are of anything we know.

Why should it matter whether or not our culture has a clear understanding of the sources of morality? Because we know in great detail the origins and character of the problems the world faces, thanks to science, and we also have some good ideas, again thanks to science, about how to ameliorate them. The failure to act on that knowledge – to take decisive action against global warming for example — arises not so much out of indifference, as a kind of moral disorientation. The loudest and most bellicose of the political voices in current media are those that deny any validity for moral standards or ethical rules, dismissing them as 'political correctness' or power-tripping élitist sanctimony. Thus, anyone claiming moral motivations – a desire to do the right thing – is by definition a hypocrite, because no such motivation can exist. In the face of this, we find it difficult, if not impossible, to make moral judgements, to say 'that is just plain wrong' or 'that is certainly the right thing to do'. The standard rejection of moral argument as 'just a subjective opinion' can be difficult to counter.

In the absence of such confidence, we are prey to the failings of self-interest, and cynicism. The forces of unexamined rationalism, the amoral cyber-corporations, the mercenary lawyers, the cynical politicians, the opportunistic religious leaders, the propagandists, all have their agendas and talking points and rationalizations, and are hard to confront in the absence of any unifying vision of a better world.

Where the convictions of faith are absent, moral realism can give each of us the courage to act on our best impulses, to do what we know to be right and to combat what we know to be wrong. And, at the same time, to understand the obligation each of us has to take up the moral conversation so tragically marginalized in western Modernity.

NOTES

1. David F. Noble, *Forces of Production: A Social History of Industrial Automation* (New York: Oxford University Press, 1984).

2. See, Roland Marchand, *Advertising the American Dream: Making Way for Modernity 1920–1940* (California: University of California Press, 1985); and Stuart Ewen, *Captains of Consciousness: Advertising and the Social Roots of the Consumer Culture* (New York: McGraw-Hill, 1976).

3. In Raymond Williams, *Culture and Materialism* (New York: Verso, 2005), 170–95.

4. See N. Katherine Hayles, *How We Became Posthuman: Virtual Bodies in Cybernetics, Literature and Informatics* (Chicago: University of Chicago Press, 1999); George B. Dyson, *Darwin Among the Machines: The Evolution of Global Intelligence* (New York: Perseus Books, 1999).

5. Rinie van Est, "Moral Shortcomings in the Technology Debate," *Next Nature* (website), last modified January 30, 2013, https://www.nextnature.net/2013/01/moral-shortcomings-in-the-technology-debate/. See also the classic exegesis by David F. Noble, *America by Design* (Oxford: Oxford University Press, 1977).

6. Ray Kurzweil, *The Age of Spiritual Machines: When Computers Exceed Human Intelligence* (New York: Penguin, 2000); Hans Moravec, *Robot: Mere Machine to Transcendent Mind* (Oxford: Oxford University Press, 1999); Neil Gershenfeld, *When Things Start to Think* (New York: Henry Holt and Company, 1999).

7. Joseph Weizenbaum, *Computer Power and Human Reason: From Judgment to Calculation* (New York: W.H. Freeman, 1976), 227.

8. Michael Polanyi, *Personal Knowledge* (Chicago: Chicago University Press, 1964), 336.

Postscript: Religion and Morality

Back in Chapter 4, we touched on an approach to morality called 'divine command theory'. This belief proposes that what is morally good (and bad) is determined by God, whose edicts are transmitted to us via intuition, revelation and the writings of specially gifted interpreters. In other words, in the realm of morality, God is the font of all knowledge of what is real: the epitome of truth. A progressive, contemporary theology has construed this as meaning that we can best approach this divinely enjoined truth by being sensitive to our intuitions (knowing ourselves) and by learning from the teachings of the specially gifted among us. And, because God has made us rational beings, we are obliged, as well, to critically analyse this information, comparing it with the perspectives offered by reason, looking for correspondences and conflicts.

One of the main activities of organized religions over the millennia has been to facilitate learning, by providing spaces appropriate to the contemplative pursuit of wisdom and by institutionalizing the processes of discovery and verification in order to expand the body of truth while minimizing the circulation of false (or heterodox) information. Holy orders and their monasteries, seminaries and convents, theological schools and universities were and are part of the process. Unfortunately, wherever it has appeared around the globe, organized religion has earned itself a reputation for the corrupt exercise of power rather than the pursuit of truth, and perhaps nowhere more so than in Christian Europe beginning in the Middle Ages.

Be that as it may, the religious approach to organizing knowledge and promoting discovery sounds a lot like the organized pursuit of knowledge through science as it developed in the sixteenth century in Europe: the new university faculties, the widespread distribution of scientific texts and the establishment of national academies of science and chartered institutions such as Britain's Royal Society (1660) and the Lincean Academy in Italy (1603). An irony noted several times in preceding pages has been the gradual transformation of science and the scientific commitment to 'objective' truth into a religion of its own, manifesting its rising hegemony through rationalist economic and political ideologies such as liberalism and market capitalism, and through the dogmatic refusal to regard knowledge accessed by means other than a reductionist 'scientific method' as legitimate and meaningful.

This tidy separation between scientific and religious truth was more or less arbitrarily settled upon during the time when the scientific world-view and its related, rationalist political and economic ideologies rose to prominence, evolving for reasons that had as much to do with the exigencies of political and economic power as any dedication to truth and meaning. Briefly put, for capitalism to achieve its destiny within the emergent liberal democracies, old-fashioned religious morality with its quaint notions of justice and equity, vice and virtue, had to be marginalized and defanged. It's a process that continues.

2

It is worth repeating that behind their respective structures of power and influence, science and organized religion, at their best, have similar if not identical agendas. Both are interested in uncovering and disseminating the 'truth' about what is 'real'. And their approaches to discovery, though they may appear at first glance to be radically different, are in many ways remarkably similar.

Most religions, it is true, have arrived at certain firm convictions that they regard as unarguable (the existence of God the Creator, the possibility of the miraculous, the authenticity of various prophets and teachers etc.), and which appear to be antithetical to science. Science, for its part, claims to be open-ended and endlessly curious, and is confident that it will, one day, have objectively verifiable answers to any and all questions about the world, including those, like the origins of the universe and life, to which religion has provided explanations that science regards as nothing more than folklore.

The apparent conflict arises out of the fact that science is focused on what it regards as fact – objective knowledge of the properties and operations of the material world – while religions are mainly concerned with value and meaning in the world. Religious 'truth' centres on meaning; the issue of meaning (in the religious sense of transcendent significance) is explicitly *excluded* from scientific enquiry, simply because it is not measurable or computable.

The contradiction in the two approaches to truth is more apparent than real, though, because there is no such thing as knowledge of the physical that is not inevitably entangled with meaning. Science studies the world by reducing it to ever-smaller component parts and collecting meticulously detailed data on each bit and piece, but it makes progress when it is able to reassemble those bits and pieces – those data points – into a whole, and recognize it for what it *is*.

What it *is*, is its meaning. The cogs and wheels of any apparatus take on collective meaning when they are assembled and the purpose of the machine becomes evident. The meaning of a watch is time as regulator; the meaning of a washing machine is cleanliness; in each case there are further levels of meaning we're all familiar with. As any object or biological entity is dissected in the laboratory, it sheds meaning at every stage of disassembly, until what is left is a collection of component parts, each of which is more or less meaningless on its own. The assembled whole is greater than the sum of its parts precisely because of the emergence of meaning. And, it should be added, with meaning emerges value, its counterpart. This insight can be observed on the scale of our own world, but it also is relevant to the entire cosmos.

3

The great defect of science, as it arose to occupy intellectual territory ceded to it by religious authority in Europe, is its refusal to accept that the knowledge it provides is incomplete, and for that reason, potentially endangering. To rely solely on its guidance can be likened to setting sail in a wooden caravel without understanding the weather, or that the world is round. Of course, the same charge of wilful blindness might have been made against medieval religious authority, which in its rigid moral and doctrinal certainties sank to brutal persecution of scientific explorers and nonconforming believers alike.

Critical moral realism as we've been discussing it in preceding chapters offers one way to reunite moral and scientific knowledge – value and fact –

acknowledging their inevitable entanglement without engaging in religious discourse; another approach is its mirror image, as set forth in what has been called critical theology, or theological critical realism.

Deeply influenced by the philosophical writings of Michael Polanyi, critical theology applies critical realism to theology

> as a way of describing the process of 'knowing' that acknowledges the *reality of the thing known, as something other than the knower* (hence 'realism'), while fully acknowledging that the only access we have to this reality lies along the spiralling path of *appropriate dialogue or conversation between the knower and the thing known* (hence 'critical').[1]

The first part of this definition is clear enough: it acknowledges the real existence of things external to ourselves. In other words, there is a mind-independent world out there that is knowable through reason and hence through science. The second part speaks to the idea that, as rational beings, we can only ever approach, and never arrive at, complete knowledge of that world because, as even science now acknowledges, there are limits to reason as a vehicle for truly comprehensive knowledge and understanding. At the same time, some things we just *know*, without being able to explain why or how (as in Begrson's *intuition*, or Polanyi's *tacit knowledge*). We feel the anguish of a wild animal; we long for companionship; we sense unseen danger, or are left breathless by beauty. Artists, for example, typically operate in this realm of experience.

Another way to understand reason's limits is to think of mathematics, reason's most highly developed and accomplished tool in terms of its ability to represent reality. A mathematical model of any system or object, no matter how detailed, can never be more than a model, a representation. And a model is not the thing, just as a map is not the territory it describes.

The way to transcend those limits to rational comprehension is through the 'spiralling path' of continuing, reflexive, conversation between the knower and the thing known – fashioning ever better, more complete representations. This path can take many forms, from scientific experiments to prayer and meditation; the important thing is that it is always open-ended, its conclusions provisional. The 'fact' it produces can be based on nothing more than consensus, whether it involves the properties of sub-atomic particles or the interpretation of sacred texts or miraculous events. For that reason, it is vitally important for the 'conversation' to be as inclusive as possible, and for it to focus on both aspects of the real – both fact and value, both the thing known and its *meaning*.

In the modern world, as it has evolved from the time of Galileo and Bacon and Newton onward, that means reconnecting, in dialogue, the disciplined learning of science and a critical realism focused on morality. It means, in other words, re-combining natural and moral philosophy in a holistic approach to knowledge and understanding.

Knowledge that cannot be communicated directly by conventional oral or written discourse is often represented in works of art and music, in myth or parables, and in meaningful ritual. In each case, the symbol refers back to a reality, and it invites the mind to seek for further evidence and clarification of that reality. A mass celebrated in a great cathedral involves many layers of symbolism intended to convey meaning in their combined expression. That meaning points back to the things, persons, and events being symbolically portrayed, and whatever power it may have to move people is derived from its deep connection with what is real. This kind of symbolically transmitted truth generally needs to be met half-way, as it were: one needs to temporarily suspend rational disbelief. For that reason, religious ritual is often designed explicitly to pave the way, to open (or empty) the mind, to prepare it for insight to come.

Michael Polanyi writes:

> [T]he book of Genesis and its great pictorial illustrations, like the frescoes of Michelangelo, remain a far more intelligent account of the nature and origin of the universe than the representation of the world as a chance collection of atoms. For the biblical cosmology continues to express, however inadequately, the significance of the fact that world exists and that man has emerged from it, while the scientific picture denies any meaning to the world and indeed ignores all our most vital experience of this world.[2]

The role of religious learning is to discover meaning, which need not be incompatible with the truth of science. Religious faith (and in Polanyi's case,

Christian faith) represents 'an eternal, never-to-be consummated hunch, a heuristic vision [...]'. [3] As with any hunch, our natural curiosity demands of us continued exploration and clarification, which takes place through a process known, somewhat unappealingly to the twenty-first-century mind, as religious *worship*. (But worship, as derived from Old English, simply means the acknowledgement of worth.)

Once again the congruency with the acquiring of scientific knowledge needs to be noted. Science as we know it is possible if and only if its practitioners maintain a faith in the unprovable hypothesis that there is an objective reality that is accessible to us through reason and its tools. It is a faith that is deeply conditioned through long education within highly disciplined institutions. In doing science, we meet nature half-way and proceed from there. In the end, truth – any truth – can only be thought of by *believing* it. [4]

Both science and organized religion serve the crucial purpose of providing a framework for understanding, a means of resolving into a sensible pattern the myriad of scattered data points encountered in daily living. As the philosopher George Santayana said, it is as impossible to be religious without having a religion as it is to speak language without having a language. [5] In both cases grammar and syntax are essential to comprehension.

4

We can safely acknowledge, I think, that without the gifts of science and the technologies it has made possible over the past four hundred years, the world would be a more dangerous, unpleasant, and less happy place for its human inhabitants than it is today. (We will set aside the condition of non-human inhabitants, including those raised for human consumption.) Could the same assertion be made about organized religion over a roughly equal timeframe from, say, the Reformation to the present? Has it, can it, make the world a better place?

First, to state the obvious, all of the great religious prophets, from Moses to Mohammed to Jesus to Buddha to Confucius, were pointing to a world beyond, to a world that reveals itself as a moral universe. It could be argued that reason does that too; that an atheistic humanism, the acme of rationalist social philosophy, may well share the same perspective. And in fact, the critical moral realism that is at the heart of this book comes to the same ultimate conclusion, or rather, accepts the same basic premise, of a moral universe.

Of course, adherence to an organized religion is certainly no guarantor of moral acuity or reliability, nor does rejection of organized religion lead one invariably down the slippery slopes of moral relativism or scepticism. But humanity in its long history of sharing a small planet has learned the necessity of constructing and maintaining institutions to preserve and promote the hard-won wisdom of experience, the principles that govern our responsibilities to one another and to the rest of life on Earth. We organize for a reason: there is power in numbers. And in organized religion, at its best, the exercise of that power is modulated by deep and continuing moral discourse anchored in faith.

Thus, while organized religion may no longer play much of a direct, day-to-day, role in modern society (certainly not in the West), it could be argued that in its implacable faith in the truth of goodness, it still serves to direct the forward motion in history. As 'progress', this is an altogether more helpful understanding than reason supplies (i.e. technical innovation and growth).

The utopia imagined in religion, whether it be the Christian Heaven, or the Islamic Jannah, or the Hindu Svarga, is not properly thought of as prediction, nor a template to be employed in the construction and management of current society; it is best seen as a reference point that offers a continuing critique of the contemporary world of human affairs, a critique of our secular utopias. In the case of Christianity, the messianic belief in the eventual establishment of God's kingdom on Earth – 'Thy will be done on earth as it is in heaven' – is intended to generate 'self-actualizing hope (not passive dependence) since the God in whom Christians believe is enabler and vivifier in history and empowers men and women to act on their own behalf. Faith in the divine promises does not make people inactive; it empowers them to act'.[6]

They act because they believe themselves to be on the right side of history. In the face of dire predictions for humanity and its only habitat coming from all quarters of science and from the humanist arts and letters, and of prospects for technological 'solutions' that threaten a hellish future in which humans and robots are blended to produce cyborg automatons, religion's message is that the future remains open and undetermined, and we should therefore not lose our nerve.

NOTES

1. N.T. Wright, *The New Testament and the People of God: Christian Origins and the Question of God* (Minneapolis, MN: Fortress Press, 1992), 35. Others in this widening community include John Polkinghorne, Ian Barbour, and Arthur Peacocke, all scientists who have seriously engaged with theology. The sociologist Gregory Baum is another.

2. Polanyi, *Knowing and Being*, 284–85.

3. Polanyi, *Personal Knowledge*, 281, 199.

4. Polanyi, *Personal Knowledge*, 305.

5. Michael Polanyi and Harry Prosch, *Meaning* (Chicago: Chicago University Press, 1975), 179.

6. Gregory Baum, *Religion and Alienation: A Theological Reading of Sociology* (New York: Paulist Press, 1975), 284.

Index